UNIQUELY HUMAN

UNIQUELY HUMAN

Raising Leaders and Creators in an AI World

AUBREY SCHMALLE, OTR/L, SIPT

Uniquely Human © Copyright 2025 Aubrey Schmalle, OTR/L, SIPT

All rights reserved. No part of this publication may be reproduced, distributed or transmitted in any form or by any means, including photocopying, recording, or other electronic or mechanical methods, without the prior written permission of the publisher, except in the case of brief quotations embodied in critical reviews and certain other noncommercial uses permitted by copyright law.

Although the author and publisher have made every effort to ensure that the information in this book was correct at press time, the author and publisher do not assume and hereby disclaim any liability to any party for any loss, damage, or disruption caused by errors or omissions, whether such errors or omissions result from negligence, accident, or any other cause.

Adherence to all applicable laws and regulations, including international, federal, state and local governing professional licensing, business practices, advertising, and all other aspects of doing business in the US, Canada, or any other jurisdiction is the sole responsibility of the reader and consumer.

Neither the author nor the publisher assumes any responsibility or liability whatsoever on behalf of the consumer or reader of this material. Any perceived slight of any individual or organization is purely unintentional.

The resources in this book are provided for informational purposes only and should not be used to replace the specialized training and professional judgment of a health care or mental health care professional if needed.

Neither the author nor the publisher can be held responsible for the use of the information provided within this book. Please always consult a trained professional before making any decision regarding treatment of yourself or others, especially in the case of internet addictions, persons with disabilities, and children with complex mental health profiles.

Some names and identifying details have been changed to protect individuals' privacy.

For more information, email aubrey@sensational-achievements.com.

ISBN: 978-0-9965653-2-5 - paperback

ISBN: 978-0-9965653-3-2 - ebook

publisher: Sensational Achievements, LLC

Get Your Free Family Playbook!

READ THIS FIRST

I know you are more likely to take action if you don't just passively consume the content of this book but actively engage with the information and take massive action.

To get the best experience with this book, download the Family Playbook for free. Print it. (Yes, paper is an important part of this journey; you'll learn more about this in a later chapter.) Put it in a folder/binder, and use it to craft a personalized family plan to raise your children to be leaders and creators in an AI world.

www.aubreyschmalle.com/uniquely-human-playbook

To my daughter—Always let your light shine for others.

Table of Contents

Introduction: Raise Leaders and Creators That Will Thrive in an AI World 1

PART 1:
GROWING UP IN A DIGITAL AND AI WORLD: CHILDREN'S REALITIES AND CHALLENGES

Chapter 1: Distracted, Disorganized, and Dysregulated Kids 7

Chapter 2: Wake Up to the New Reality of the Digital World .. 17

Chapter 3: Why the Time Is Now 25

Chapter 4: Reality Check: I Feel like an Island 49

Chapter 5: Do I *Really* Know the World My Child Is Growing Up In? 61

Chapter 6: Is the Answer Just Limiting Screen Time? 93

PART 2:
THE FIVE PILLARS AND YOUR PERSONAL PLAN

Chapter 7: Pillar 1: Save Yourself First.................................... 117

Chapter 8: Pillar 2: Connect and Collaborate 135

Chapter 9: Pillar 3: Move with a Purpose 153

Chapter 10: Pillar 4: Learn and Grow Sensationally................ 173

Chapter 11: Pillar 5: Build Digital Awareness and Safety 209

Chapter 12: The Winds of Change Are Blowing..................... 233

Endnotes 241

Acknowledgments 265

About the Author 267

INTRODUCTION

Raise Leaders and Creators That Will Thrive in an AI World

There are two words that describe good parenting: firm and kind.

—Dr. Daniel Amen

I would like to congratulate you. Picking up this book already shows that you are an intentional parent. You are someone who cares not just about coordinating the schedule to get to the next soccer practice, making sure the kids are fed, and following the bedtime routine. If you are a parent of a teen, you aren't just focused on college applications or attending sporting events. You are a concerned parent who wants to raise successful children who are ready to enter into a world where technology has forever changed the landscape of how people interact with one another, the way that products are sold, the way we do banking, the way that we monitor our health, the way we do business, the way we educate, and the way each of us conceives of our own selves. The list could go on and on. We need to prepare our children to thrive in the AI world of tomorrow by the intentional decisions we make today in the way we raise our children.

The Intention

This book's intention is to help you better understand the collision of technology, the new normal of living with computers in our pockets, the growing impact of artificial intelligence on the opportunities our children will have in the world, and how children develop. From there, this book outlines how to use Five Pillars to create success habits for your children to thrive in today's tech-entrenched AI world. With this book, you can learn how to be a more intentional parent with numerous tools to support your children to become empowered and independent leaders and creators, not passive consumers and followers of algorithms.

Who It Is For

This book is for every adult who spends time with children. It's a book that will help you understand the challenges and opportunities available to all of us as we navigate the world of screens. The habits kids need to succeed in a digital world are not just about learning how to use technology. They are about priming the brain's pathways for academic and career success, fostering development, building communication and relationship skills, and helping children learn how to better balance screen-based activities with movement for a healthy and happy life.

Why Listen to Me?

In this book, I draw from my personal and professional experiences, as well as from lots of research. I'm a single parent of a Gen Z daughter. I am also a pediatric sensory integrative occupational therapist with my own clinic, Sensational Achievements, LCC. I have seen over a thousand children in my 20 years of practice and consulted with over 26 school districts to optimize support for learning and self-regulation for children with diverse neurosensory profiles. I am constantly learning and researching not only about brain and body development but also human behavior, family dynamics, and the most current shifts and trends in our society, in particular the impact of screen time on children. Never has there been such a time in history where the world is changing so rapidly with so little guidance on how to respond as parents.

Also, in this book I draw from history, science, economics, the arts, current events, pop culture, and academic studies and research to aid you in developing a nuanced picture of not only the challenges of but also the opportunities in and success habits for guiding your children to skillfully navigate the world of screens.

The Book's Setup

This book is divided into two parts. Part 1 focuses on the way life in a digital and AI world has impacted family dynamics and our children's lives. The aim is for us to better understand our children's particular realities and challenges, which are quite different from what we grew up with. With Part 1 as the foundation, we then move to Part 2. This is where you'll encounter the Five Pillars, which you'll use to formulate habits and routines to empower your children in today's technology and AI world. With these success habits, your children will learn to operate in life empowered and independent, as leaders and creators, not passive consumers and followers of algorithms.

Additionally, the free Family Playbook allows you to process your thinking around critical messages and ideas in each chapter and put together a customized plan for how you want to enact changes in your home so that everyone thrives. You can download this playbook at www.aubreyschmalle.com/uniquely-human-playbook.

As parents in today's ever-expanding digital AI world, we can no longer take the advice of our parents or even recycle the things that we learned as kids. Also, if we believe our own parents were too authoritative, we can't just do the opposite and be extra loving to our children, so our children know we care. We want our kids to be financially independent, experience success in college and their careers, be emotionally strong, have healthy relationships, make good choices, live independently, have strong identities, and have digital literacy. These desires for our children, however, are often at odds with our day-to-day routines and the opportunities available to our children if we don't intentionally cultivate them. The secret is balance, boundaries, and opportunities. These are the key elements of any healthy relationship with others and with our screens. And all of this we'll explore closely in this book.

I hope all those who read this book will be inspired to raise their children intentionally, so they can be happy, healthy, and successful in an AI world, harnessing their uniquely human abilities. When the new habits for living in an AI world become part of your family's lifestyle, your children can pass them down to their kids who, undoubtedly, will have even more technology innovations at their fingertips.

Part 1

Growing Up in a Digital and AI World: Children's Realities and Challenges

For many parents, we grew up in a world where we still had to go to the library to put together a research paper. There were no digital menus. No packages or flyers that said "Scan Me" to access a video, manual, or coupon in order to figure out how to set up an entertainment system or save a little money at checkout. There was no "Tap to Pay," and we still had to carry around quarters for the parking meter. Ordering fast food required that we call the restaurant for delivery or go up to the counter and ask for a "number four, supersize."

Now the world encourages us to engage with technology first and people second. Technology guides us toward consumption of products, media, and solutions to every problem. All we have to do is hit the "easy button"—just another app on our phones. This means our children are growing up in a world where human connection and social opportunities are being disrupted along with the opportunities to solve their own problems so that they can be the leaders and creators of tomorrow's AI world. Technology has been embraced across all aspects of life from shopping to learning to healthcare to socializing. But at what cost to the well-being of our children?

In Part 1, we will explore how the goals we have for our children to be happy, healthy, and successful in life are at odds with the current digital world that strives to build more consumers than creators. We will also discuss how the COVID pandemic catapulted us into this digital world but why you as a parent are in a unique position to raise your children to thrive by creating your own family playbook that Tech Giants can't manipulate once you understand the challenges your kids are facing.

CHAPTER 1

Distracted, Disorganized, and Dysregulated Kids

*To be a parent is to be chief designer of a product
more advanced than any technology and more
interesting than the greatest work of art.*

—ALAIN DE BOTTON

Over the years, I have gotten more and more distracted and disorganized. This spilled over into who I was as a mom and a professional. My ability to complete projects and paperwork in my business, clean the house, feed my child something somewhat healthy, figure out how in the world I was going to get her to activities and support her in her interests—all while I was also juggling 500 million other tasks—were all impacted. Did I mention that everything had to happen between the hours of 5:30 a.m. and 11:30 p.m. if I had any hope of getting at least six hours of sleep? As a single working mom, I have to admit, it is completely exhausting. The more technology has become a part of my life, the more I find myself in a perpetual state of stress and distraction, being pulled in many different directions all at once.

As she was growing up, my daughter communicated to me on more than one occasion that she didn't feel like I had enough time for her. She needed more time with me, but it always felt like every urgent thing was important. It wasn't. All she asked for was my time, which I seemed to have too little of to give. Now considering I was already experiencing this the year the iPhone came out in 2007, I can only speculate what today's parents of young children are experiencing as smartphones have become the center of our day-to-day lives.

My daughter's babysitter introduced her to the joys of Candy Crush and other online games. Luckily in my own home, the iPad that she had access to was outdated and did not have many games on it. She had many more other activities she preferred to do, including practicing gymnastics and building extravagant add-ons to her dollhouse like a ski lift made out of string, straws, and cardboard. Watching her do these things always reassured me she was generally on the right track—even if I couldn't spend as much time with her as I would like and she did play video games now and then.

COVID: Isolated and Screen-Bound

During the pandemic, we found ourselves with more time than ever on our hands. For me, it was an opportunity to reconnect with my daughter as a mom because my business died overnight. I was lucky enough to have forced extra time on my hands to learn how to play pre-beginner tennis, get better at ice skating, take long walks, and meet up with friends outside while socially distancing. Not every parent working from home or deemed an essential worker had that same opportunity. It only happened for me because the government told me I could not open my private practice to see clients. Apparently sensory integration therapy wasn't that essential. In hindsight, that was the opposite of true for children who had no sports or after school activities, but safety was the top priority. Even when I returned to my clinic, clients were slow to come back; their parents understandably weren't certain they would be safe in an environment where other children were playing.

However, as work picked up and my daughter went back to school on a hybrid schedule as a middle schooler, she had many, *many* hours to herself spent in front of the TV or playing games on an iPad. While she could usually be found doing some sort of arts and crafts simultaneously, the TV was always on in the background. She even decided she would pick up baking as a new hobby. Good news—this eventually led to a cottage baking business. Bad news—I had to accept the reality of finding chocolate on every handle in the kitchen. I still felt terrible as a parent, worrying what was going to happen given the amount of time she was not spending in school and in after-school activities as she had been doing before COVID. I had concerns about her mental health and her development. There really didn't seem to be a workable solution.

Not only am I a concerned parent of a Gen Zer, as already mentioned, I am a sensory integrative pediatric occupational therapist with my own clinic. For over 20 years, I have specialized in evaluating and treating children who have differences in the way that they process sensory information from their bodies and from the environment. Some kids have learning disabilities like dyslexia and dysgraphia. Others have developmental delays, autism, or attention deficit disorder. And then there are those that fall in the gray area with no diagnosis but are still struggling to adapt to the world around them. Having this background made me acutely aware of all the daily multisensory learning experiences that children were not able to get during the COVID shutdown. When I say "multisensory learning experiences," I'm referring to how we take in the world through our senses, using that information to adapt and respond to the demands and invitations of the world around us. This is the process that facilitates learning and development. (We'll be talking about this in greater detail in Part 2). In that shutdown, there were so many missed opportunities for social connection that were replaced by going to school via Zoom and Google Meet or just completing assignments posted in Google Classroom followed by hours of downtime in front of screens on social media or playing video games. Many children are still trying to recover from the impact.

The Mental Health Crisis That Followed the Pandemic

In 2015, I created the Body Activated Learning™ Framework,[1] outlining movement activities that children need to improve attention and learning in the school environment. For children who are neurodivergent, it could also be utilized as part of their home programming with support from an occupational therapist. Little did I know that five years later, children would be thrust into a world of isolation and excessive use of technology. When the way we did life drastically shifted from in-person to screens, we got to see what a world of isolating ourselves away from other people and sitting in front of computers, phones, and iPads could do to us … and our kids. Many parents had children that suffered academically, socially, and emotionally during the height of the COVID pandemic. After the shutdown was over and my practice started to come back to life, my new clients presented with significantly more behavioral, mental health, and learning needs than I had previously seen. Children commonly refused to go to school, experienced social anxiety, and struggled to learn in a classroom environment.

It was clear. A life of isolation, internet scrolling, online learning, asking Siri, and gaming instead of going out into the community to engage with others was a recipe for the now-identified children's mental health crisis that followed.[2] But five years later, it has expanded rather than resolved. This awareness was the beginning of a new mission for me and the reason I wrote this book. I speak to teachers, administrators, and parents about the challenges kids face growing up in a digital world. I run workshops with kids and parents, encouraging face-time interaction (not the Apple FaceTime app!). The programs help kids understand that technology is a bit like a McDonald's Happy Meal: While it tastes good, there are some healthy things in it, and we would love to have it every day, too much isn't good, and there are many hidden dangers.

After one middle school talk, the administration implemented a tiered response to inappropriate smartphone use. In a matter of weeks, they saw a significant shift in the social dynamics and social media issues arising in school. In fact, schools across the country are finally reevaluating how much technology they are using and whether or not to allow smartphone use during the school day. Not to mention that, beyond the social impact, ChatGPT and a myriad of other AI tools are finding their way into student assignments, making new rules even more critical.

A parent shared with me that their family's shift into rebalancing screen-based and real-world activities started with a power outage. After 24 hours of complaining, her children rediscovered their musical instruments, started creating new buildings with their Legos without a step-by-step manual, and were much more engaged with the family. It gave her the motivation she needed to decide what long-term shifts she wanted to make in her family routines to keep the changes going. Another parent's journey began when her child threw the iPad and broke the screen. She reported her son's emotional regulation issues and difficulties communicating his emotions both at home and at school shifted more quickly with the supports he had in place when screens were no longer an option.

The number of distracted, dysregulated, and disorganized children has risen to a level that our society can no longer ignore. It's time for change. But it will take a village of educators, parents, and community agencies that support children to help our children thrive in a digital and AI world. I am certainly a member of that village, and I've written this book so that you and so many others can join as well.

Fighting Against the Tech Giants

Legislation—the Kids Online Safety and Privacy Act—has been introduced at the federal level in an attempt to hold companies like Meta accountable for the content that children under 16 are able to view.[3] It has been passed by both the Senate and the House as of July 30, 2024 but is still undergoing revisions and has not been enacted as I write this book in 2025. In creating this legislation, congress members pointed out that online platforms for both gaming and social media significantly contributed to the rise in depression, anxiety, social comparison, and eating disorders. Meta's initial response was to expect that parents with children under age 16 give permission for downloading the apps. In anticipation of this act, social and gaming platforms have been reevaluating their current policies and parental control features. If you are a parent of a tween or teen, you probably already know that a child who wants to access an app has no moral problem changing their birthday on their device to be able to get access. You may also know that "family sharing" on iCloud allows children to download any app that their parent already has downloaded, so if a parent has social media, then their children can easily and independently get it as well.

As parents, we are often told to limit our children's screen time, not just because of the content and online predators, but also because of the impact it has on learning, behavior, and development. This is a challenge given that, for middle schoolers and high schoolers, most social interactions occur online. These experiences can be both good and bad. According to Common Sense Media, 26% of tweens ages 8-12 are spending four to eight hours per day and 29% of teens spend more than eight hours viewing entertainment media.[4] This increase in middle and high school is exacerbated by the introduction of Google Classroom, advanced placement course videos, SAT prep materials, and online textbooks. Internet trolling is a common vice for both adults and children, some of which is now cultivated by AI chatbots. If your children aren't victims of cyberbullying or internet trolls at some point, they may be at risk of becoming trollers. Research published in the *Journal of Child Psychology and Psychiatry* in 2022 shows that in 9- to 11-year-olds, frequent social media screen use led to a 62% higher prevalence of conduct disorders. Large amounts of television, video game playing, and texting increased the likelihood of developing oppositional defiance disorder by 21%.[5]

We have reached a crisis level when it comes to the health and happiness of our children. While it may take many years for laws and safeguards for children on the internet to evolve, we can do a lot as parents right now to acknowledge the fact that our children are growing up in a world that we never experienced, influenced by internet users from all walks of life who are trying to increase the number of consumers of their products, who design content for adults that children can access, or who may have negative or criminal intentions. Big Tech's AI innovations are fast taking the human out of social interactions, making it normal to watch AI-created videos and interact with chatbots over people. It's the Wild Wild West, and there is not really a rulebook for how to approach it for adults or children.

This Is Your Chance

We all want our children to be happy, healthy, and successful. But sometimes that is at odds with the direction a consumer-driven economy is guiding us. It's not just the research that is telling us it's time to rethink our relationship with technology. It's our children's day-to-day behavior—like tantrums when we take the iPad away or constantly asking for our phones if they don't have one of their own—that screams *we are out of balance.*

Is technology embedded into most aspects of life for kids? Definitely. Is the answer "limit screen time" in an AI world and your kids will be fine? Nope. That's a losing battle. Screen time will inevitably increase as children grow and an increasing number of tasks can only be done digitally or require interactions with AI to be accomplished. Do we need to find new habits and routines that work for an AI world and give our children what they need to thrive? I argue yes.

Daily life experiences of both children and adults are forever altered by the presence of technology. It opens up a world of knowledge that previously could only be read in books and newspapers. It allows us to experience people, products, and events at lightning speed any hour of the day or night. It pushes people and businesses to figure out ways to be noticed and relevant. But it also impacts our interactions with family, friends, and coworkers. It affects how we learn and the types of activities we are engaged in. It encourages more people to be consumers than creators and innovators. It changes kids' daily social experiences to be more online and out of view of parents, and it affects children's knowledge of socially appropriate behavior as well as expectations about how the world works.

This book offers you the opportunity to learn how to proactively teach your children success habits that will help them to thrive in a digital and AI world. It's not too late to begin making these changes, no matter how old your children are or whether they have specialized needs. It requires a shift in your lens to understand how your children are experiencing the world and the key foundations necessary to help them develop, capitalizing on the unique multisensory way that the brain and the body learn. Don't worry. As I said, I will help you with this part.

This is a brave new frontier for parents—the Wild Wild West. I will be your guide, but you can't afford to wait any longer to take action for the benefit of your children. Some of you are already seeing your children struggle socially, emotionally, or academically. Others have young children who have yet to be introduced to technology because you already have a healthy fear of its effect on your children even if you are using AI daily in your life and work. Whatever your stage in your parenting journey, I promise that there is value in what I am about to teach you. As humans, we are always growing and changing. If we learn from our mistakes, we can blaze a path forward to help our children become empowered and independent leaders and creators, not passive consumers and followers of algorithms.

No matter where you stand on the pros and cons of technology, we will cover all your objections in Chapter 2. Change is hard and arguably doesn't happen overnight. This journey is about progress, not perfection.

> Download the Family Playbook at aubreyschmalle.com/uniquely-human-playbook before moving on to Chapter 2. Print it (yes, paper is an important part of this journey; you'll learn more about this in a later chapter) and use it to craft a personalized family plan to raise your children to be leaders and creators in an AI world. Complete the exercises for Chapter 1 before moving on.

CHAPTER 2

Wake Up to the New Reality of the Digital World

*My children, of course, will have a computer,
but first thing they will get books.*

—BILL GATES

As technology has embedded itself in almost every aspect of our lives, it's easy to see that many of the "old ways" of doing things are just not available. Gone are the days where high schoolers carried around a 50-pound book bag with all their textbooks. Gone is the 100-foot phone cord stretching from the kitchen into a closet where kids hid from their parents to have private phone conversations. Cubicles and rows of filing cabinets in office spaces are being replaced by open concepts and digital file folders on a shared network, or no office at all with the advent of work-from-home. Checking in at the laboratory clinic for blood draws is done via touch screens and QR codes rather than talking with a receptionist. Schools communicate with parents via message apps that send information in soundbites rather than filling a student's bag with colorful flyers that fall out when it is time to get out the homework folder. Contactless payment has made it easier than ever to tap your life savings away at Starbucks. How many of us still carry enough cash around on a daily basis to pay for items we need as we run errands? How many businesses do you know that are still closed on Sunday besides Chick-Fil-A? Do you still write letters or mostly emails, including the occasional obligatory thank-you note? Slowly, your own habits of engaging with the world have shifted as you have become a consumer in a digital world.

What's Your Personal Opinion on Technology?

Chances are that even if you initially struggled to learn each new process, you accepted the gradual creep of technology into your home, your children's schools, your workplace, and your community. Some of us not only accept it but get really excited with each cool piece of technology that seems to make life easier. You may be the first one to get the new iPhone or only lease cars so you always have the most up-to-date technology. I have to admit, I am pretty curious about the shopping carts that scan and tally up what you have purchased, checking you out automatically on the way to the car. Haven't tried them—but I am curious how they work.

Where do you fall? Are you skeptical about how much of your data is being collected every day? Are you worried that AI will take your job? The release of ChatGPT and many other AI platforms made that a reality for many industries starting in 2023. Or do you see technology as a place of constant innovation not to be feared but to be embraced? Maybe you are somewhere in the middle. I think most of us are. "The middle" is a pretty big place with lots of variations in opinions on the right ways to use technology. As parents, we are always asking ourselves how we should use technology but also how we should let our children use technology. And arguably, screen use creeps in more and more—as life gets busy and we get overwhelmed; as we are seeking learning and communication solutions; or as what we or our children need is just not available offline.

Ah, the Good Old Days

Like our parents and grandparents before us, you may already find yourself repeating the timeless phrase, "When I was your age…" We may not have the story of walking to school five miles uphill both ways, but Gen X parents did grow up pre-smartphone. Callers had to leave messages on our answering machines and wait patiently for us to return phone calls. Millennial parents had technology integrated into their academic life much more regularly as young adults. For those born in the '90s, use of technology in the average household grew steadily during the dot-com boom. Many parents from this generation exposed their children to technology earlier because they experienced the positives of connection, collaboration, and impact as the opportunities available online grew. No matter what generation you belong to, we are all raising our children the best way we know how in a constantly changing world filled with technology.

We can all agree that the world keeps shifting. Naming some of those shifts puts you in a much better position to decide what changes will have the most impact for your children and adapt your parenting strategy accordingly.

This book focuses on the beliefs that:

- You are a parent who wants the best for your children, so they grow up happy, healthy, and successful.

- What is best for your children and what the world wants you to believe are not always the same thing. You have to find your way through the noise and make the best decisions you can along the way.

- How you set up each day—being proactive not reactive—sets the foundation for your children's health, happiness, and success in life.

"But, Aubrey, This Seems Like You Are Asking a Lot"

I am asking a lot. I do have high expectations. But I also have a very strong belief that you are reading this book because you are a parent who cares, a loving parent, and a parent who is just trying to figure all this out—the same way I am. The only difference is that I have experiences in my professional toolbox that have shifted my lens and the way that I see the challenges that kids are facing. I am committed to helping you shift your lens too.

My whole life I have told myself, "I am too overwhelmed and I don't have time." I said this when I didn't go to the gym. I said this when I opted to serve chicken nuggets and French fries at dinner for the fifth day in a row. I said this when I was too tired to take another trip to the playground, and it was just easier to let my child play on the iPad while I finished another evaluation for a client.

We have all been there. Most of us are still there and will continue to be there for many years to come. That is both the joy and the challenge of parenting. We somehow make it through, and our children continue to grow and develop in spite of us. I didn't learn until my child was a pre-teen that a lot of what was holding me back was myself and my own habits. During the pandemic, I read the book *The Miracle Morning* by Hal Elrod. In it, he outlines what he refers to as the SAVERS method, an outgrowth of research on the habits of highly successful people. It was my first step towards setting up habits and routines for myself that would eventually pay dividends for my child. If you are interested in hearing more about his work, Amazon and YouTube will be happy to introduce you.

How Success Habits Can Transform Children's Lives (And Yours)

In this book, I am going to walk you through the Five Pillars that, when cultivated, will help your children succeed in an ever-changing digital world:

- Pillar 1: Save yourself first.
- Pillar 2: Connect and collaborate.
- Pillar 3: Move with purpose.
- Pillar 4: Learn and grow sensationally.
- Pillar 5: Build digital awareness and safety.

These are the Five Pillars around which you will create success habits and routines to help your children be leaders and creators in a digital and AI world. I have witnessed many children whose lives have changed as a result of cultivating these habits and opportunities in collaboration with their parents. I often invite parents into my sessions, so they can see how I guide their children toward understanding themselves and the world around them for lifelong learning. Parents see how I help kids find their "bravery brain" and get out of their "worry brain," so they can confidently explore the world around them and become resilient.

Kids learn flexibility, cooperation, and positive communication that allows them to adapt to many people and situations, expand their creativity, and move out of their comfort zone all through opportunities to experiment, practice, and develop mastery over their bodies and their environment. Parents learn the language of empowerment so that they can help their children understand what works for their body, what helps them get ready to learn, and when they need to take time to recover. They learn how to set up activities and create opportunities within the environment while maintaining a strong belief in what's possible for their children to achieve. The habits you will learn are simple, actionable, and designed to be flexible enough to meet the needs of your family, regardless of your children's ages. You will be better able to create opportunities for critical experiences that foster brain and body development while keeping in mind the skills that leaders and creators need to have that can never be outsourced to AI, securing the opportunity for your children to succeed in an AI world.

Some of the Benefits

Here are a few of the benefits you can expect to see in your children when you implement the Five Pillars of Success in this book:

- Improved behavior and self-regulation
- Increased exploration, awareness, and engagement in learning

- Enhanced adaptability for greater independence, flexibility, and executive function skills
- Expanded social skills and ability to connect with others

I should add that when I write, "executive function skills," I'm referring to the skills of self-control, planning/organization, goal setting and follow-through, flexible thinking, and reasoning and problem-solving that so many children struggle with today in the "done-for-you" world of AI and technology.

"But, Aubrey, I Am Terrible at Sticking with Prescriptive Programs. Life Is Too Hectic in My House"

I know these are big promises, but my goal was to create a book that is purposeful, actionable, and customizable to your unique family dynamic without telling you to limit screen time or prescribe a daily routine that is a "must do" for every family. Achieving balance is not about what you limit, it is about how you spend your time. I am going to help you make a Family Playbook to take immediate action towards setting up your environment, your family routines, and your new expectations. It is my hope that you will have an active conversation with your family, especially if your children are older, and collaborate to find a balance that fits the unique rhythm of your family's life. If you make too many changes too quickly, you might set yourself up for failure. I believe you can win. I believe you can begin to make the changes necessary to make success habits part of your children's everyday experiences.

Whether you are a parent who is exhausted and overwhelmed or a parent who is high performing and highly organized, you will learn how to cultivate success habits for your children. It doesn't even matter if your children struggle with learning disabilities, ADHD, behavior issues, difficulties with executive function skills, or are on the autism spectrum.

We are all sensory beings, uniquely human, who rely on information from our bodies and the world around us to learn and grow. The key to fostering growth in your children is in how you help them balance technology with other multisensory life experiences. Achieving this balance optimizes the way the brain and body were meant to learn while supporting self-regulation. The result is happier, healthier, independent, and successful children. This is the dance that I will teach you.

> Pull out your Family Playbook, and complete the Chapter 2 exercise.

CHAPTER 3

Why the Time Is Now

I choose to live by choice, not by chance; to make changes, not excuses; to be motivated, not manipulated; to be useful, not used; to excel, not to compete.

—Miranda Marrott

This is the part of the book where I throw out some scary facts and figures to impress upon you just how important it is to consider the habits and routines that you are going to build into your family going forward so that your children can thrive in a digital world rather than fall victim to it. Remember, the goal is for you to support your children to become empowered, independent leaders and creators, not passive consumers and followers of algorithms in an AI world.

The Mismatch

We all share common desires for our children, but the statistics show that there is a mismatch between what we want and what is actually happening in our children's lives.

- **We want our kids to have emotional and mental well-being.** According to the National Institute of Mental Health, 31.9% of youth ages 13 to 18 have had an anxiety disorder.[1]

- **We want our kids to have healthy relationships and social skills.** An online survey of 6,000 children and parents revealed that 54% of children felt their parents spent too much time on their smartphones and 32% felt unimportant when parents were using their phones.[2] A study of 325 teens and adults ages 14 to 80 found that smartphone usage leads to reduced social connectedness, which then promotes more smartphone usage.[3]

- **We want our kids to experience academic success.** A 2018 study funded by the National Institute of Health showed that MRIs have found significant differences in the brains of some kids who use smartphones, tablets, and video games more than seven hours per day. Kids who spend more than two hours per day on screens got lower scores on thinking and language tests compared to those who spent less than two hours or none at all.[4]

- **We want our kids to have digital literacy, internet safety, and make good choices.** In 2023 the National Center for Missing and Exploited Children reported that child exploitation online increased on Instagram, Google,

TikTok, Twitch, Reddit, Omegle, and Discord.[5] Reported cyberbullying was at 46% in 2022 for teens ages 13 to 17.[6]

- **We want our kids to live independently and manage daily tasks.** Quizlet, a global learning platform, released a survey in March 2024 showing nearly one in five recent high school and college graduates are the least confident in handling automotive maintenance, such as changing a tire or the oil. This is followed by financial planning (17%), insurance (12%), minor home repairs (11%), cooking (11%), cleaning (8%), and organizing (8%). They wished courses had been offered in these subject areas or had someone in their lives who taught them these things.[7] The internet never sleeps. As life has gotten busier, productivity expectations have increased. The space and time to engage in many of these activities as adults alongside children to foster learning and life skill competency has shifted, with many parents forced to trade time spent cleaning or fixing cars in the driveway with time answering emails and getting on Zoom calls.

- **We want our kids to achieve financial independence.** Seventy-nine percent of recent graduates on the same Quizlet Survey said financial planning overwhelms them the most. Twenty-nine percent of respondents said it negatively impacts their mental health. While we can't say that screens are solely responsible for this gap in financial education, financial education begins early in life as children watch parents exchange money, balance a checkbook, or make bank transactions. "Tap to Pay," online shopping, and online banking have made much of this process happen out of sight of children, giving the illusion that money comes in infinite supply as Amazon boxes and dinners are delivered to our doorsteps.

- **We want our children to have job opportunities.** A 2024 survey by Student Voice noted that college students graduating in the next four years want to be taught critical thinking and problem-solving skills that will help to make their jobs AI- resistant.[8] In 2022, Forage, in partnership with Knit Research, surveyed 1,000 students pursuing a four-year undergraduate degree at a US college or university. Sixty-five percent of college students said understanding how industries and companies work in the real world is very or extremely important to them, but only 30% said they are very or extremely satisfied that they have the tools or information to do this.[9]

As children grow into young adults, they are beginning to question how knowledge presented in coursework and tested on the SATs in high school is preparing them to offer more value and skills to a company than AI is offering. They have been told in school that information can be easily searched online and does not need to be memorized. But it is the retaining and manipulation of knowledge, applying it to real-life experiences, that builds the reasoning and problem-solving needed to be hired for AI-resistant jobs.

- **We want our children to be confident and have a strong personal identity.** The 2023 Girls Index by ROX, a survey of more than 17,500 girls in fifth through 12th grades, offers a glimpse into how young girls' experiences are affecting their mental health, confidence, and relationships. Those who used social media for ten hours each day were 25% less likely to describe themselves as confident when compared to girls who used social media for less than two hours per day. It also found that, compared to 2017, the percentage of girls who report feeling confident has dropped from 68% to 55%, and that girls in fifth and sixth grades experienced the largest declines in confidence and self-perception.[10]

In a social landscape of direct messaging, group chats, sharing posts, and responding to friends' posts, children learn to adjust their behavior to gain approval from others. While this is nothing new for the middle and high school years, fitting in has become a public event, with large numbers of peers, even those kids don't know, weighing in on what they see in a post rather than getting to know each other on a deeper level and forming supportive and healthy relationships.

- **We want our kids to be successful learners.** The National Center for Education Statistics reported that in the 2022 to 2023 school year, the number of students ages 3 to 21 who received special education and/or related services under the Individuals with Disabilities Education Act (IDEA) climbed from 6.4 million in 2012 to 7.5 million in 2023.[11] From 2016 to 2023, identified students in need of individualized education plans increased by a half million while public school enrollment declined from 50.4 million to 49.5 million.[12] This is likely due to a combination of enhancements in medical technology, people having babies when they are older, environmental factors, and societal shifts leading to disruptions in development. As a country that values inclusivity in public schools, we strive to educate students of all abilities in a general education classroom. Without a clear way of doing that, technology accommodations and educational games become an easy, even if not ideal, solution.

While it may be tempting to blame many of these statistics about kids' lack of (or perceived lack of) basic life skills on an educational system in dire need of an upgrade (and I don't disagree with this), there is much more to it than this. Skills for life are built and reinforced through everyday experiences even if they are introduced at school. For example, learning how to figure out change on a worksheet means nothing if you don't actually practice making change at the store, right? Learning social skills evolves from thousands of opportunities for face-to-face interactions beginning in childhood. When we engage with the world through technology and AI solutions, we outsource and automate many of the tasks that our brains and bodies need to do to develop critical social skills, reasoning, problem-solving, learning, and proficiency in many different areas of life. So, due to technology, the way we "do life" has fundamentally shifted, and these statistics are proof of the consequences. We will dive deeper into this as you learn more about the Five Pillars of Success in Part 2.

Why I Can't Stay Silent

As a pediatric sensory integrative occupational therapist, I have studied extensively how the brain and body work as well as the factors that contribute to self-regulation, learning, attention, and adaptability. My personal and professional experiences have been so significant that I know that I can't stay silent. While I never really got into video games or social media posting, I still find myself perpetually distracted when I jump down the rabbit hole of the internet, watching endless

YouTube videos while trying to teach myself how to be a better parent, a better entrepreneur, and a more successful business owner. There was a period in my life where I signed up for newsletters, took courses, and listened to endless podcasts on my drive from one appointment to the next. I spent more time doing this than exercising and being present in the world. I learned a lot, for sure, but I also consumed way more than my brain could possibly retain and take action on. I will never get those hours back. In hindsight, it was basically a lot of daydreaming about what I wished to accomplish but never actually achieved. Like starting (and failing at) a new diet—I was overwhelmed with the volume of information. Then what I learned I should do and what I actually did were not in alignment.

While I will always have a love for learning, I learned that my life is exponentially richer and more fulfilling when I make time for face-to-face interactions with others, exercise, pause to put into action the things I am learning, and allow myself to be fully present when I am with my own child as well as with other people's children. Learning is nothing without action. It's easy to consume high volumes of information but much harder to internalize and integrate it into our lives. Getting out of "urgent" and focusing on "important" is critical to progress.

I am lucky that my child did not have access to social media when she was young and only got an Instagram account after she turned 16. While I know she missed out on some social interactions because of it, I dare to argue that her current friendships are much richer and deeper because she has the skills to be fully herself when socializing at school. Not being online created time and space for those skills to develop in face-to-face interactions. Her online interactions are an extension of her real-life experiences rather than a replacement for them or a constant chasing of "likes" for validation.

In my practice, children often provide more insight into their screen use than parents do. They say things like, "I'm really tired today. I woke up last night, and I couldn't go back to sleep." When I ask them what they did instead, they often say they found the iPad and either started playing games or checked to see if their friends were online. The older ones have sometimes commented how surprised they are to see how many of their friends are also not sleeping. I bet that most parents were fast asleep in their beds with no idea that their children went online in the middle of the night just because they couldn't sleep. Having gaming consoles in their rooms is another recipe for building social interactions and experiences centered around an imaginary world where they can be the heroes of their own story, playing endlessly at all hours of the day and night away from the prying eyes of parents.

I have other child clients whose every play idea and discussion centers around a video game they play or watch someone else playing on YouTube. It's like their brain has been hijacked by entertainment media, and they have no other real-life experiences to talk about. For some of these kids, it doesn't matter how much their screen time is limited. They are drawn to screens as a replacement for a world that doesn't make sense. Even in small doses, it quickly becomes all they can think about—a place where there are immediate rewards and "done for you" experiences that they can just consume. No imagination needed. Just earn virtual money to buy things at the shop built into the game.

Neurodiverse Children Are Vulnerable

Several studies suggest children who are neurodiverse are much more likely to struggle in school, struggle with forming friendships, and struggle with their self-esteem as they have trouble keeping up physically with their peers.[13,14,15] It's not surprising that many of them are drawn to a fantasy world where they can feel powerful and good enough; this is exactly the imbalance that is so dangerous. Children who struggle in real life socially, academically, or motorically are much more vulnerable to the dangers that are present in a screen-based world. Research shows that neurodiverse children often have overlapping diagnoses such as speech delays, autism, dyslexia, and developmental coordination disorder.[16] The deck is stacked. It is up to us to ensure that our children develop the skills they need to succeed and thrive in a digital world to become the leaders of tomorrow. The more children experience the negative effects of living in a screen-based world, the more vulnerable they become to developing mental health issues that keep them from being independent and successful.

We can stop the progression of this mental health crisis for our children. But we need to work together. We need to understand how they experience the world and what we can do to guide them so they feel empowered, competent, and successful. And, yes, that's one of the big aims of this book … and of my life.

What Changed for Me

The best part of my recovery from the COVID pandemic was the opportunity to tune into the things that my child needed to grow into the amazing young adult that she is today. We both added in regular opportunities for exercise. We each make time to focus on connecting with each other while also processing the challenges of life. We support each other in our passions, and she may have been one of the few teenagers that asked advice from her mother (sometimes) that she then passed on to her friends. She bluntly would tell her friends, "If I know, then my mom probably knows too, and maybe she can help." I don't say this to suggest that I am a supermom. Believe me—I am no such thing. And there is no "perfect family."

I say this to show you what intentionally cultivating a relationship with your children can look like and the peace of mind that it can bring knowing your children feel they can come to you for guidance rather than seeking advice from a stranger or chatbot online.

Our First Challenge: Overwhelmed and Exhausted

If you poll 20 moms, you may get 20 different answers for what they feel the biggest challenge is they face day-to-day. But the overwhelming complaint from parents in my workshops is exhaustion and feeling like they have too many things to do while not really knowing how to make sure that their children are productively occupied. Many families in America have two working parents and may still be struggling to get by. The cost of living continues to grow. A 2024 Bankrate survey showed that more than 34% of those responding were just covering their living expenses with nothing left over, which categorizes them as living paycheck to paycheck. Fifty-nine percent said that they are uncomfortable with their level of emergency savings.[17] This means prioritizing work and earning income over quality time with their children so that they can provide for them.

Aside from financial pressures, many parents struggle to figure out how to arrange childcare to manage days off from school. They often sign their children up for one-day and two-day camps if they do not have a relative or babysitter available. Additionally, parents struggle to manage downtime for their children, often feeling like they need to schedule their children for adult-led activities such as sports practice, dance class, art class, and after-school programming to ensure that their children are both safe and occupied while also engaging in their passions and interests. For some children, this leads to feelings of being overscheduled and overwhelmed with no bandwidth left for doing homework. Many schools have cut down on homework for this reason. Is this good or bad? Are we more or less connected to what our children are learning in school than even ten years ago?

As parents we are also overbooked and overscheduled, trying to answer emails, send text messages, and post on social media to stay connected with our friends and family. Between work, appointments, and running the kids to all the activities we have signed them up for, we grab 30 minutes in the waiting room to catch up on emails, pay bills, or make some progress towards a work deadline. For myself, sometimes I purposely don't immediately answer text messages. Not because I don't care about the person who sent me a message. I just can't think about whatever the message entails at that moment. Just because it was on someone else's mind, doesn't mean it should be on mine at that moment. At first, I felt horribly guilty because I didn't want people to think I didn't care. I am not going to lie and say some people didn't get their feelings hurt initially. Now, I am pretty upfront in telling people that is not the case. I am truly trying to be present with what I am doing, and sometimes that means that I can't get back to someone for a few days.

We are only human and can only accomplish so many things in one day. Keeping that pace of productivity can be exhausting. We often don't have the capacity as parents to guide our children at the end of the day to help out with chores and make dinner when it would be faster to just do it ourselves so that we can check it off the list. Plus, our children are also often exhausted at the busyness of their own day, looking for downtime … in front of a screen.

Stay-at-home moms and dads also find themselves overbooked and overscheduled as their partners work long hours to provide enough income for the family. Stay-at-home parents are rarely at home either. They are the people that schools rely on to join the PTO, volunteer in the community, and join committees. There is no one lifestyle that is easier than another because we never lack for things that could be or must be done in a digital world of constant connection.

"You Are Making More Work for Me, Aubrey!"

Les Brown says, "Do what is easy, you will have a hard life. Do what is hard and you will have an easy life."

This is a quote that I often share during my speaking engagements and workshops because it rings true both in my own life and the lives of the families that I serve. Change is often difficult because it's out of our comfort zone. It's not the way that we were raised. It takes conscious effort in the beginning. I promise you, consistency leads to automaticity. We are all creatures of habit. That is why it's often so difficult to embed new habits into our lives without boundaries and triggers to make them happen. The brain relies on repetition to form and strengthen connections that help us to respond differently as we get older and expand our life experiences. We live in a world that thrives on consumption, not repetition. Until those new connections in the brain form, it's easy to revert to our default settings when things get hard.

Cultivating new habits for both yourself and your children involves:

- Starting off with a strong morning routine
- Setting up physical boundaries in the environment that will help your family succeed
- Adding things to the environment that create opportunities for your children to engage in multisensory, non-screen activities to foster growth and creativity
- Harnessing the features available on smartphones and tablets to help your children manage their total screen time and make positive contributions to the world while also knowing the limitations
- Guiding your children daily to balance screen time with meaningful face-to-face interactions

Our Second Challenge: Determining the "Right Things" to Do

We have been told for years that our health depends on proper diet, exercise, and sleep. Whole health and wellness industries are more than happy to sell their version of how to get there through packaged exercise programs, vitamins and supplements, and if necessary pharmaceutical intervention. These are just the products for adults, but what about our children? The American Pediatric Association (APA) is now recommending a balance of face-to-face interactions, time outside and away from screens, exercise, sleep, and nutrition.[18]

I never thought that I would see the day when we specifically had to tell parents to prioritize face-to-face interactions. However, now that screens have disrupted this key way to connect with others and learn to read facial expressions, it is becoming necessary to remind parents of the importance of this human experience.

The Five Pillars in this book will help you cultivate success habits for your children to manage screen time, connect with others, increase their multisensory movement opportunities for self-regulation and learning, and safely navigate online experiences.

I don't expect you to work miracles although you will start to experience them as you implement changes little by little. I just ask that you take the strategies that are most actionable for you and leave the rest to add later as your family adjusts and starts to see the benefits. It's pretty weird as a child to wake up one day and feel like all the rules have changed and the routines that you have lived with until now are suddenly different. That can be very dysregulating, so I don't advise that you try to do everything at once. I do advise that this journey should begin with a conversation with your family in a way that everyone can understand and get involved in setting up. Keep in mind that while some of the strategies you implement as you raise your children will change form with age, the principles are applicable to children, tweens, teens, and adults alike.

Habits That Led to My Transformation

Before I even realized that screens were playing a key role in disruptions and disorganization in my own life, I spent a lot of time learning about the habits that high-achieving entrepreneurs use to help them succeed. Highly successful people seem to give the same advice but in different packages. Hal Elrod's book is evidence of this. Most only give advice to adults, and there is no real guidance on how to translate this to children.

Whether you are listening to Tony Robbins, Hal Elrod, Jim Kwik, or (insert your favorite coach or entrepreneur here), there is a generally accepted, uniquely human short list on how to succeed, and it typically includes the following:

- Hydrate, eat right, and sleep.
- Exercise.
- Breathe.
- Express gratitude.
- Create space to focus.
- Visualize.
- Read and learn.
- Take action.
- Celebrate victories.
- Recalibrate, adapt, repeat.

Seems easy, right? Right … more like easier said than done. Just keep reminding yourself that success is a journey, not a destination—for you and your children.

Many also note that wealth is not only financial. It is also wealth in relationships and wealth in health. If I had to identify my three main roles in life, I would say occupational therapist, mother, and business owner. When my ability to earn income was suddenly taken away with the pandemic shutdown, there was no easy way to shift to earning enough income to support myself and my child. Luckily, there was assistance for businesses to help us survive even if it came at a cost of long-term business debt. The only choice I had was to embrace the other parts of my life—be the best mom I could be given the situation and spend more time engaging in activities that improved my overall mental and physical health. Rather than letting myself fall down the rabbit hole of fear and worry like many people did, I focused my efforts on what I could control. What I realized is that I'd been chasing financial "wealth," but it was way out of balance with other critical aspects of my life. I'd spent more time working and trying to earn money than I had on my personal health and on building my skills as a parent. Fast forward five years later, and I will tell you without even thinking that those critical moments in time, even though the future was very uncertain, showed me why people often say you need balance.

Balance is not the same for everyone. Admittedly, I had difficulty trusting that if I implemented success habits in my own life, my business wouldn't go under and that I would still be able to support my child. I "didn't have time." I had too many obligations and too many bills. This type of thinking is mostly fear-based. And it is out of alignment with what humans are capable of achieving when we "optimize our wiring." Jim Rohn, a widely-respected personal development speaker, once said, "Your level of success will rarely exceed your level of personal development because success is something you attract by the person you become." This has become a guiding principle in my life. My personal development, no matter how many YouTube videos I watched or podcasts I listened to, lagged behind what I wanted my success to be in life. I was out of alignment, and I was letting my fear and overwhelm drive most of my decisions. It took completely losing control of the certainty of the future of the business that I had built before the pandemic to create space for me to take massive action in the other areas of my life where I needed to grow.

Fast Forward to 2025

I still have bills to pay and SBA EIDL loans from COVID on the books. But in all of my life, I have never been so aligned with my own values and needs. I am connecting more with others in my community than ever before. My growth as a parent, friend, community member, and business owner has brought me more in alignment with the person I have always felt I was meant to be. As I have come more into alignment, I have built wealth in all three areas of my life. I have shifted out of being overwhelmed daily by investing in my continued personal growth and contributing more to the people I love and my community. I am busier than I have ever been in my life. I now speak to parents, educators, and professionals who serve children on the impact of living in a screen-based world. I train other therapists to reimagine their treatment strategies to meet the needs of neurodiverse children. I work to inspire and empower others to shift their lens through which they view the behaviors of children growing up in a digital world while helping design home strategies, school initiatives, and targeted interventions that better meet the needs of this unique generation of learners.

I still use technology ***a lot***. I have a smartphone, two iPads, three computers, a dual monitor, video lighting and equipment, a TV, and a smart home security system. I would be lying to say that I live a "low tech/no tech" life, but it would also be a lie to say that both my child and I aren't thriving despite and because of the relationship we have with technology.

I have come to realize, no matter how much I have on my plate, being overwhelmed is just a feeling. But if my success and happiness are driven by having "wealth" in all three categories, then intentionally making changes to the daily habits that I model and foster in my own home exponentially increases the chances that my daughter will go out into the world and cultivate "wealth" in her own life. Am I a millionaire? On paper, maybe not. But the answer to that question all depends on your perception of wealth.

Habits That Led to My Child's Transformation

Whether the decisions I had to make as a parent were popular or not in the moment, my daughter has benefited from the unconditional love and guidance I have worked hard to learn how to communicate. She also benefited from me modeling habits of success—watching my growth as it relates to friendship and health, seeing me help others, and watching me work toward my goals. I am proud to say that she has learned uniquely human lessons:

- Having friends is conditional on being a friend and reaching out.
- Exercise is important for mental and physical well-being.
- Helping others brings joy and impact.
- Academic achievement can open doors to other opportunities.
- Figuring out who you are as a person is more important than just people-pleasing.

Her habits reflect these lessons. They were initiated by her with my modeling, support, and encouragement. Her friendships are genuine. She plans study sessions and how she wants to exercise. We have daily "facetime," so we can share our days with each other. She makes sure that her Instagram feed is populated with cute puppies, positive life advice about health and wellness, and things that make her laugh. She has learned the scroll strategy of "if you don't want to see more of it, don't watch it in the first place." If you do, make sure to scroll by it quickly next time and instead—find a cute puppy. Her behavior tells the algorithm she doesn't want to watch anything upsetting or depressing. I trust that she has enough tools in her own toolbox to share with me if something doesn't look right. She trusts me to guide her in her responses when necessary. She actively uses privacy settings and blocking features. Her friends share their locations to keep each other safe and stay connected. As a young child, this modeling and educating was my parental responsibility. I definitely failed, but our family is proof that it's never too late (or too early) to start the transformation process.

If Jamie Can Do It for Her Son, You Can Too!

Jamie was a mom that I met in 2016 whose child, Jason, was outright refusing to go to school. Academically, Jason was a high performer. He also had a diagnosis of high-functioning autism. In middle school, he was overcome with anxiety about navigating the hallways, changing classes, and meeting the expectations of a new level of independence. He was a lover of video games, using it as a way to connect with friends. At first, his mother thought that it was a good thing because he was connecting with other kids and he had some friends. As the anxiety and overwhelm feelings kicked in, video games became all-consuming. They became a way to escape from the challenges of real life into a place where he felt successful and happy. Then Jason had a week off school for winter break, and there was nothing that

Jamie could do to get Jason back into the classroom afterward. For the next several months, they met with school counselors and many other professionals to complete evaluations that would lead to a plan to address the problem. In between, he stayed in his room playing video games. Much like an addict, it got to the point where he wasn't even really having any fun. His daily life was filled with worry and anxiety. Leaving the house became harder and harder. He also was not getting an education and was not spending time around other kids his age. After our evaluation, where he refused to do any activities that involved movement and preferred to just sit in the chair completing activities at the table, his mom and I had a conversation.

Luckily, I was connected to an occupational therapist at a therapeutic school that was well versed in sensory integration and also very good at working with middle and high school students. As Jason prepared to transition to this school, his mother needed a lot of support and coaching to limit his access to his computer for the duration of the school day until he was willing to get in the car and make his first trip to a new school that was ready to receive him with love and support. After opting to do his lessons in the car while sitting in the parking lot on the first day, he eventually walked through the school doors and began participating in both academic activities and a customized exercise program facilitated by my colleague.

Two years later, he was ready to transition to a school that had adaptive gym classes and larger class sizes. By the end of his middle school years, he had developed a love for fencing, was working with a personal trainer, and was invested in his exercise routines. He told his mom that he wanted to go to a magnet high school in his home district. His relationship with technology had improved significantly. He no longer only played video games with his friends but was able to throw a ball around outside, walk to the local convenience store, and hang out with friends while talking about events and people in his life.

In our interview, his mother said she learned a lot about how to support him, but she still had "PTSD" from the time when he refused to go to school, suffering alone in his room in front of his computer. While she could not do it alone, she found the support necessary to help him through this difficult period. He went back into a typical high school with no accommodations in place. He exuded confidence and purpose for the first time in his life. He was the one telling his mother not to worry about him and that he was going to be fine. That would not have happened if he hadn't had the emotional support of a village while adding in movement activities and life skills that allowed him to become confident in his body, so he could develop interests outside of the computer. Jason's journey gave him the foundations for success that allowed him to show up in the world, learn, grow, and develop relationships with others without overwhelm.

Relationships for a Lifetime

It's hard to get kids off of my caseload. Many families don't want to give up their time slot for fear of not being able to get it back. While I don't think that children should spend their lives in therapy, it reminds me how much both the children and the parents value the self-esteem and empowerment that comes along with a child feeling safe in their body and in the world. It reminds me how valuable it is to have people in your life that can "see" your struggles and guide you through them. I try to be that person, both for the children I serve and their parents. When a child I meet for the first time does everything possible not to leave the clinic after an evaluation, it was probably one of the few places that child started to feel safe and happy. My goal for every child, no matter their age, is to feel empowered and supported as they grow into the best version of themselves.

I am only one person, but I want as many children as possible to experience having someone in their lives who is their "biggest fan and supporter." I want to share my tools with you so that you can cultivate that relationship with your child. The Five Pillars will help you achieve this. In doing so, you will be able to approach your children with compassion, understanding, love, and empowerment as their guide towards a life of "wealth" fueled by success habits that are uniquely human.

Is This Just Another "Five-Step Process"?

Nope! I wouldn't do that to you. I can tell you from personal experience that a "five-step process" only works for the select few that have a similar lifestyle to the person they downloaded their free toolkit from. (Full disclosure—this is how my inbox got overrun with automated emails until I spent 20 to 30 minutes daily deleting them all and **not** working on the "five steps to … whatever").

The Five Pillars that are introduced in this book show you how to implement success habits that meet key developmental needs and allow your children to become the leaders of tomorrow. Our old habits and routines don't work anymore. Some are worth keeping, and some need redefining. As you fill out your Family Playbook, you will be the one redesigning your family routines away from a one-size-fits-all social expectation to a journey towards raising your children to be adaptable, resilient, life-long learners with the uniquely human skills to thrive in a world that changes at lightning speed. I will teach you how to prepare your children's environment to naturally foster boundaries and exploration. I will teach you how to be more mindful when you are interacting with your children. I will help you understand why fighting your own "mama bear" or "papa bear" while letting your kids fall and fail (but being there to dust them off and try again) is actually one of the most compassionate and loving things you can do for them.

Parenting doesn't come with an "easy button," and change is hard. It is normal to experience a lot of false starts. It's normal to feel alone in your journey even if you joined an online support group to try to keep yourself motivated. In the next chapter, we will discuss how to acknowledge your own humanness (not a character flaw but an asset) and set yourself up for success as you strive to raise leaders and creators in an AI world.

> Take out your Family Playbook, and turn to Chapter 3 to reflect on your current family habits and begin setting goals to help your children succeed.

CHAPTER 4

Reality Check: I Feel like an Island

If it takes a village to raise a child, it takes a village to support that child's parent.

—Ann Douglas

Sometimes I feel very alone in my parenting. As a divorced single parent, I unfortunately could not find a path toward co-parenting as I had hoped. Children who live in two different households sometimes struggle to navigate the differences in parenting styles, and there may be nothing that can be done to help them reconcile that. Sometimes the same is true within a two-parent household. There may be one parent who is often checking their phone and working constantly on their laptop while the other takes on the role of getting kids to activities, helping with homework, and making sure everyone eats. This story often repeats itself in school as well. One year, a child may have a teacher who has a more disorganized and chaotic teaching style and the next year have a teacher who is an expert at classroom management and supporting the diverse needs of students in a classroom. Kids are exposed to different adults with different styles of interacting throughout life. It's impossible to completely control the experiences children have each day. However, many years of parenting, working in pediatric therapy, and listening to motivational speakers helps me remember that one positive and consistent force in a child's life who guides them and models behavior can still make a huge impact. To not try is a bigger mistake.

Consider the Story of Les Brown

I quoted Les Brown earlier in the book, but maybe you have no idea who he is. Let me tell you about him.

In his speeches, Les says that he was labeled "educably mentally retarded." One day he met a high school teacher that changed his life. The teacher asked him to go to the board and write something down. Les said he couldn't. When the teacher, Mr. Washington, asked why not, Les said, "Because I am educably mentally retarded."

Mr. Washington responded, "Don't ever say that again. Someone's opinion of you doesn't have to become your reality."

Les Brown never forgot that and still retells this story almost every time he speaks. That moment changed the path of his life, and he started believing in himself. While the path was not smooth, he started living life with a "why" and a purpose. He is now an international speaker.

The point is—life is made up of many moments. Not every moment will be happy. Not every moment will be perfect. Not every adult will be a positive and supportive influence in a child's life. Children start to figure that out when adults come into their lives who believe in them and push them to become the best version of themselves. You can be the light—the one who shows up consistently and predictably to help your children succeed at life. Not every response you give will be perfect. That's okay. You can help them build resilience, adaptability, and discernment so that they can make choices that will empower them to succeed. You are playing the long game. Progress is never perfect, but I assure you—your kids are listening and watching you. Your presence as you strive to raise them with skills to thrive in a digital world will not go unnoticed (even if it feels unappreciated sometimes).

Sometimes, as parents, we feel like we are on an island getting little to no support from friends, coworkers, family members, spouses, or even our children's educators. You try to limit the time your child spends with technology, but the world is adding more digital kiosks and educational apps by the second. Not everyone is reading the same playbook (or even reading at all). The fight can be exhausting. The positive thing about the digital world is that we have a choice to seek out spaces that will help us grow and thrive as parents and to cultivate those spaces if they don't readily exist. To do that, we have to keep a few truths in mind about what it is like to parent in a digital world.

Truth 1: In a Connected World, Many of Us Feel More Alone than Ever, Including Our Children.

Adults and children alike seek approval and validation through "likes" and shares on social media, yet the algorithms on social media are designed for increasing ad revenue, with us, the viewers and engagers, as the product being sold. This means that influencers will always get more views. Because anyone can post, our post may be seen for about a minute, unless we are posting multiple times per day. It's easy to get caught up in trying to get feedback and validation from friends, peers, and strangers on social media. At the same time, our circles of friends that we spend quality time with and rely on for support are often getting smaller and smaller. At the end of the day, I don't know many people who comment even six months later about how many "likes" and views one of their posts got (unless it went viral). The posts just fade into the sea of social media.

For 13 years, I barely spoke to any neighbors on my street. I lived in an area of rented condos and multi-family homes. I am sure there are many people who live in areas like this or in downtown apartment complexes, but it seems like when you live in places with higher populations, everyone's personal space bubble is much smaller. Prior to moving to what I thought was a smaller suburban city, I lived in New York City. There, your personal space bubble may only be about two inches from your body on a crowded subway. You do your own thing, bury your head in your phone or listen to music just so people know that you aren't staring at them and you have no need to be their friend. (Because, of course, you have your own friends, right?)

I now live on a street where the moms get together for a book club. There are block parties. Kids and families go outside for walks as soon as the weather is nice. My dog, a blonde, 20-pound poochon, is very social. We jokingly call him "Mr. Mayor" because he seems to only want to go on walks to meet every person and dog who is outside at any given moment. If he doesn't see anyone, he stages a sit-in, as if I am supposed to sit outside with him and wait for a social opportunity. And as much as I laugh at his behavior, he is a great reminder that community and real-life interactions, rather than those on social media, are much more likely to make good memories and create connections with those around us. I can say that I am absolutely happier; my child is happier. It has led to getting to know more people, to getting invited to more backyard fire pit gatherings, and my daughter getting babysitting jobs or getting hired to make cakes for birthdays and baby showers.

Not everyone is going to have a neighborhood like this. But there are always opportunities to show up in person and make connections. Joining a Zoom parent meeting at school is not the same as creating an opportunity for impromptu side conversations with parents after the PTO meeting. Volunteering to be on site for a community event is not the same as sending out flyers and emails. While both jobs are important, creating opportunities in your environment to connect with others often leads to networking opportunities you don't anticipate. In today's world, we may see someone's name on an email list for months and never meet in person. Looking for activities to do with your children that give them a way to meet and interact with diverse people is an important life skill that can't be gained from a structured playdate or sports team. And it gives you an opportunity to guide them in building social skills and learning about safety with strangers, which is critical when they start going online. You don't have to be an island. If we all seek out more opportunities to engage face to face, pretty soon the "likes" and shares don't seem that important because we are experiencing true connection, purpose, and value in our communities.

Truth 2: It's Easy to Put Parenting at the Bottom of the List in a Connected World. We Bought Into the Marketing Message That We Need to Make Everything "Faster" and "Easier" Just to Be Able to Get Everything Done.

Most of us are overscheduled. We have so many groups and events that have requested our participation that we sign up with good intentions but rarely make it to the event unless we know some of our friends or relatives will be there and are expecting to see us. Family dinner is a rarity in many households, depending on what time each activity starts or ends and how long it takes to travel. Many parents are so busy it just feels "faster" or "easier" to do things ourselves like dishes and laundry rather than involving our children. Because we have created that structure and expectation, our children complain and whine rather than rising to the occasion. The cycle begins.

We cave. We find ourselves giving our kids tablets and smartphones to watch videos and play games more than we should, so we can focus on the task at hand (driving, laundry, dinner, scheduling playdates …).

We feel guilty about too much screen time. We feel like we are too busy to spend time with our kids. We tell ourselves we are bad parents. We try to convince ourselves it's a necessary evil.

We move onto anger and resentment. "Why am I stuck doing all this stuff and no one is helping me? Why am I dealing with *another* tantrum when I tell my kids to get off the tablet? Why can't they just listen? Why do they have to annoy me?"

We bargain and try to find a quick solution. "Okay, I need to limit screen time." We tell the kids to go play. We sign them up for more activities. We tell ourselves we have to keep them busy, so we can also get our to-do list done.

We cave. When it doesn't work and the kids are still irritable and whining while we are trying to get things done, everyone gets into a bad mood. We cave again. Back at square one.

Let's be real. It's exhausting. And our kids don't seem to be better humans because of it.

Present Parenting Doesn't Have an "Easy Button"

We have been sold a lie that there are faster and easier ways to do everything. But it seems that all that has done for us is make parents and kids more stressed out, looking for quick rewards that only give temporary relief. As Albert Einstein said, insanity is doing the same thing over and over and expecting different results.

So what if we shift our mindset as parents? What if we create intentional structure, accountability, and space for positive feedback? What if prioritizing parenting actually gives us less stress, more joy, more connection, and more independent children?

I encourage you to shift your lens away from simply focusing on limiting screen time to understanding the way life in a digital and AI-driven world is changing family dynamics and childhood experiences, the focus of Part 1 of this book. Once you understand that, I will share with you the Five Pillars grounded in science and research (the focus of Part 2), so you can be intentional with how you choose to guide your children toward success.

Truth 3: People Say They Want to Change, But It's Not Easy.

A 2019 study in *Science* revealed that the average completion rate of online courses is 5% to 15%. If it's a massive open online course, that number is more like 3% to 6%.[1]

A 2022 article by Matthew Mason on LinkedIn[2] suggested that it could be due to a few factors:

- Limited structure
- Limited interaction, support, and feedback
- Limited accountability

I would say from my personal experience: check! check! and … check! I always have good intentions. I have even paid higher prices because I thought it would make me more accountable to completing the course. But the reality is that the structure and human factors are critical when you want to help someone succeed. If I didn't specifically connect with anyone in the group, it was easy to skip online meetings. If I didn't meet a deadline, it was easy not to schedule a call with my coach, and they didn't really chase me to do it. They did chase me to buy the next product though—a summit, mastermind, or whatever the next sale was. All that did was reinforce my own belief that they cared more about my money than my success.

Interestingly, the same goes for our children. They rely on us for structure, supportive interactions and feedback, and accountability. If we want to empower them, we have to give them space for independence and inspire them to succeed with the right tools, structure, and accountability. This is not about raising the next doctor or lawyer. Maybe that's not the career your child was meant for. It's about creating space for success in ways that lead to a life of wealth in all areas while living in an AI world.

We all want our children to be happy and successful, but there is so much confusing advice and information out there it's overwhelming, and we often tap out before we get started or fall back into old habits after a week or month. If that wasn't the case for most things people do, we would not see variations of the same New Year's resolution magazine articles, advertisements, blogs, and social media reels every January. As you read this book, I don't want you to join just another course that you probably won't finish. I do want to offer you a chance to build opportunities for community and connection, both in real time and with a wider online community. This can only happen if you invite friends on this journey with you and share this book with others. Who cares if you sign up for an online class or support group if it doesn't have a direct impact on the way you and your children experience life?

It's Time to Commit

Now that you have heard the three truths and the sobering statistics of children growing up in a digital world, it's time to commit. Most people are likely to end up stuck in the same self-defeating cycle of being overwhelmed, worrying, quick fixes, and quick failures. But now it's time to make a decision about what *you* will do differently if you really and truly want your children to grow into empowered, responsible, and happy adults that can effectively navigate and thrive in an AI world.

Are you ready to commit? Are you ready to no longer accept that your children are likely to become statistics for anxiety, depression, or bullying at some point? Are you ready to no longer accept that a screen-induced version of ADHD is inevitable? Are you ready to no longer accept that with AI taking over writing, designing, and customer service, your children are doomed to struggle to find well-paying jobs and become financially independent? Are you ready to accept that the path our children need to succeed currently cannot be found in consumption of AI tools and knowledge alone but in creation?

The reality is that if we don't change, our kids won't change. I know you love your children and would do anything for them. I also know that we did not grow up in a digital world filled with AI. The strategies our parents used don't necessarily apply. We genuinely have it harder as parents because there are almost no physical boundaries in place to protect our children from the downside of living in a screen-based world. Our only choice is to get educated and take action. Not tomorrow. Not next week. Now.

Maybe you are thinking that your children are too old and you have missed the window, or you are saying to yourself that you are already stuck in a negative dynamic with screens. I am here to tell you it is never too late to show your children how much you love and care for them. Parents are imperfect. But if you commit to growing and draw them into the journey with you, they will grow too. My proudest moments were when I saw my daughter come home from a day of working with tweens at a summer camp and she is telling me all the strategies she used to guide them. She tells me how she knows they trust her because they seek her out when they need support and when they want to play. She is out in the world making her own impact, and I think to myself, "All those years, she really was listening!"

I confess, I really had no idea if she was or wasn't listening when she was young, but I tried to keep modeling positive behaviors anyway and hoped for the best. You can help your children create an extraordinary, uniquely human life for themselves. While it may take some time and hard work on your end, it pays dividends long after your child moves away from home and maybe even for your grandchildren who will also be born into a world that changes faster than humans can adapt.

To help ensure success, I recommend that you surround yourself with other parents who are committed to empowering their children to lead happy and successful lives in a digital world. It takes a village. Cultivating one in your own neighborhood is the best way to build a community of shared values and expectations. You can support each other, encourage each other, and best of all, complain to each other. All while pushing each other to the next level in your parenting strategies. It's challenging when your children are the only ones in the friend circle who aren't accessing a phone or tablet all day or your friends only interact through social media and texting. If you can cultivate a circle of like-minded parents, your children will also be surrounded by peers growing up in similar home environments that are striving to raise their children to succeed.

Even if you have a friend or relative who has interest in this concept but is scared to take the leap, this is your opportunity to be the person who adds value to their life and the lives of their children. This can only make it easier to implement the strategies you will learn in this book because you will be cultivating a community that can support you rather than just fighting against the current of smartphone use, media in education, and screen-based parenting.

In order for you to be ready to start this journey, you need to answer this next question in Chapter 5.

> Start building your village by reading this book with another parent or small group. Use your Family Playbook to brainstorm. Not sure who to ask? Harness the positive powers of the internet to send out DMs or ask people you know to go to aubreyschmalle.com/uniquely-human-chapter to check out *Uniquely Human* and grab a free chapter to see what it's all about.

CHAPTER 5

Do I *Really* Know the World My Child Is Growing Up In?

Technological progress has merely provided us with a more efficient means for going backwards.

—Aldous Huxley

As much as I think I know, I admit I am learning right along with my child. I remind myself that I grew up in the age of file cabinets, answering machines, encyclopedias, drinking from the garden hose, and Saturday morning cartoons. I had dial-up internet in high school. Instant Messenger emerged as the way to stay connected with friends, but you had to sit down at a desk to do it. Texting wasn't a thing. There were natural physical boundaries that created space for the human things of life. Specifically, boundaries between the desktop computer, socializing, and getting my schoolwork done.

My child was born the year the iPhone was released, but because I was never one to have the latest and the greatest, tablets and smartphones didn't find their way into my house until she was about five years old. This meant she was still using the library (renamed the "media center") in elementary school and did not get a tablet and Chromebook until middle school when the COVID pandemic demanded them. Reading and math games were assigned for homework in elementary school but were optional. I opted out and spent quality time with my child instead.

For those of you who had children even just a few years after me, your children may have Chromebooks and tablets in elementary school. Your children may have smartwatches. Your children may have a close relationship with Alexa or Siri. Artificial intelligence has now exploded on the scene as a major disruptor to all industries and business structures in less than a year even though it has been evolving slowly since the 1960s. I just made a Pinterest vision board with my daughter. She was appalled that I actually wanted to click on the tiles and read the articles rather than adding something to my Pinterest board based on just the photo. A professor of a media class at a university in Colorado told me most college students report getting their news from social media in one-minute soundbites from many different sources. My generation still goes to major news websites to read the news. Maybe it's because we still had a newspaper of our choice delivered every day when I was growing up that we believed were trusted sources. Either way, it seems reading has taken a back seat to pictures and videos in a digital world.

At this moment, you might be thinking, "You are stating the obvious, Aubrey." I agree with you. You know all these things are out there. You probably use a lot of this technology. But you use it with a lens of how it makes your life easier and more efficient. Some of us see technology as a mostly positive thing. Others of us prefer to use it as little as possible to protect our privacy or preserve our sanity. But we have the benefit of having grown up in a lower-tech world, watching our parents write checks and pay for things in cash, learning how to wait for food at a restaurant, carrying a 20-pound backpack full of textbooks, and having to have whole conversations with people when we met or talked on the phone. As these daily opportunities have shifted, there has also been a significant shift in the way children experience the world. It isn't just the presence of technology. It's that we do life differently. Little things that set the foundations for our own human development are not the daily experiences of our children without a conscious effort from us.

There is no official parent handbook. With your first child, you probably read a lot about development and were watching for all those developmental milestones just in case something wasn't right. But what still hasn't made it into those books is that those milestones are actually a reflection of the brain's ability to process information, make sense of the world around us, and adapt to its demands or invitations. This is even more critical than the milestones themselves because it sets the foundation for growth and development. Good news: By the end of this book, you will have as close to a parent handbook in your self-authored Family Playbook as I can give you while saving yourself a lot of internet research. Let's start with what we do know about the experiences of our children today.

We Fill Our Time with Phones

Parent-child interactions have shifted. If parents are shopping, their child may be in the stroller or shopping cart looking down at a video on a smartphone or tablet. Sitting at a restaurant, I can usually count more than five families waiting for their meal who have children watching online videos. Walking behind a father-daughter pair who was in front of me in the coffee shop checkout line as we go back to our respective cars, I see him latch the car seat restraints, take his phone out of his pocket, and give her some time to watch her favorite video on the five-minute ride home.

Doing something on our phones has become a way to fill time when we need to wait for something else to happen or to keep us entertained if we are doing something else less desirable. In the past, many people would read books or magazines, knit, or chat with another person in the waiting room if they knew they would need to sit more than ten minutes. It would be naive to say that people didn't look for ways to pass the time even before smartphones. However, while we may be catching up on work emails, scheduling the next playdate, or reading an e-book, we are still on a screen. And our children have no idea what we are doing. All they know is that it's not paying attention to them.

I was recently talking to a teenager who said that he didn't really feel he knew anything about his dad. I told him just the other day, his father said when his phone sent a notification during our meeting, "It's not important. Just my friends messaging me," to which this teen responded, "Friends? My dad has friends? I have never seen them!" This response reminded me how common it is for us, adults, and our children to be in separate worlds. For our children, there is no indication of what we are thinking about or what is going on in our life because all they see from the outside is "your phone is more important than me." Author and speaker Simon Sinek speaks about this as it relates to interactions we have with other adults as well. Even when we make the effort to put away our phones and be present, we find so many others around us buried in their phones that it's easier to return to the status quo than strike up a conversation. Having your phone next to you on a desk during a team meeting signals to others in the meeting that they aren't the most important people to you. Sadly, this is playing out for middle and high schoolers in their school cafeterias as well during a prime period of development for social skills. Being on a screen sends the signal that you are not interested in connecting with anyone in person, even if that person is sitting right next to you.

Reflexively, many of us offer screen time to our young children during transitional moments as well. It helps them sit longer, they are less disruptive in restaurants, and they are less likely to wander off or throw a tantrum over toys that we pass by in the store on the way to get more socks and underwear. It's easy to use smartphones and tablets like a "digital pacifier" with young children. The problem with that is that children then do not develop the self-regulation capacities they need to recover from disappointment and build resilience.

The one time both children and adults are more or less forced to put down devices is when we are doing something that requires both hands and active engagement: playing a sport, going swimming at the beach, or being part of a theater production. This is easier said than done though. When I led a screen-free interactive parent-child workshop at an elementary school, 50% or more of the parents immediately went to their phones when they saw that a teacher would be leading the activities. When they were the ones who were leading, 25% still had their phones on the table within view just in case a notification came through.

If we want our children to develop healthy relationships and social skills, our own device use is something to start paying attention to. When we thoughtfully use our own devices, we set the foundation for connection and collaboration in our children.

We Embraced the Concept of "No Line, No Wait"

I remember when Burger King used the slogan, "Have it your way." It was so well known that when kids wanted to say to someone that they didn't get their choice, they would say, "This ain't Burger King. You can't have it your way." The more important thing to take away from this is that we used to accept that you can't have everything exactly as you want it. Sometimes you have to compromise. Sometimes you have to wait your turn. Sometimes as the supervisor, you get to make an executive decision, but hopefully for the greater good of the company. In a digital world, entertainment apps like Hulu, Netflix, YouTube, and Spotify allow everyone to *have it their way*. Companies tell us that as long as we have personal devices (phone, tablet, laptop), we can listen to what we want and watch what we want. In an attempt to increase their revenue, these platforms are showing more and more ads and require an upgrade to get rid of them. *Don't want to see ads? Good news! You can pay us more and you don't have to!* Even this promise has turned out to be false as ads find their way into each level of service eventually, but the allure of the comfort of getting what we want is ever-present.

Those of us who remember when we had to sit through ads while watching TV may be able to deal with that as a minor annoyance and a chance to go to the bathroom or get a snack while others have to have the upgrade. The reality is still that, aside from the ads, you get to choose what you want to watch and immediately switch to something else if you don't like it because it's "on demand." Yet we are shocked when our children struggle with patience and demand things from us, following up with tantrums if they don't get them. Gone are the days when you waited all week for the Friday night movie to be played on your favorite TV channel or waited six months for the movie that you saw in the theater to come out on video so you could watch it again. Gone are the days of listening to the car radio or watching TV as a family with the usual fights about whose turn it was to pick a show or the radio station. As long as you have your own device, sharing and patience are unnecessary.

We love having choices. It makes us feel more in control of our lives. We love to lean into things that give us autonomy. As humans, we also thrive in structure and routine, but we need novelty to learn and grow. Being faced with adversity and experiences that force us to cooperate or wait our turn builds patience, perseverance, and communication skills. When these small opportunities to compromise and learn how to wait are practiced through daily experiences, it creates space for children to build on these foundations as they develop into adults. While these opportunities still exist in school and at birthday parties to some extent, the option to retreat to an iPad or computer is still there for most children. Connecting to a screen has become a much more rewarding and easier choice for kids than socializing with their peers. Skill development disrupted.

If we want our children to have more job opportunities in an AI world, the ability to connect and collaborate with people while fostering creativity and innovation is critical to competing for jobs. These are uniquely human skills that can't be outsourced to AI.

Academic Learning Has Changed

Schools Love Google Classroom

In schools across the country, Google Classroom is the main way that teachers post assignments and provide information to students since its inception in 2014. Chromebooks are one of the most cost-effective solutions to create a way for children to access online learning content. Many schools now provide every child with a personal device starting in fourth grade or even younger. These devices allow children to access information quickly. Kids have learned how to use their creativity to code video games, make graphic design projects, and build slide show presentations. However, I can tell you from many school observations of kids across Connecticut that kids are very good at tabbing between Minecraft and the work they are supposed to be doing. They are also good at spending an excessive amount of time changing the font and searching the internet for images instead of writing content for a report. If the work feels hard, distractions are readily available. My daughter told me that the way they messaged each other in class in middle school was to share a Google Doc with their friends and delete it at the end of class. There are programs such as GoGuardian available to help teachers monitor children's online behavior during class, but it's not done in all schools and does take up additional time that the teacher could be spending walking around the room and engaging students in the learning process. While Chromebooks may have reduced copying and textbook costs, the cost-benefit is debatable when they also become a vehicle for distraction.

Gamified Learning as a Solution for Leveled Learning in Integrated Classrooms

In a 2024 systematic review published in *Frontiers of Psychology*, researchers and educators recognized the potential of game-based learning to enhance engagement, motivation, and learning outcomes in early childhood education.[1] Gamified online reading and math programs have been a way for teachers to provide "leveled learning" to neurodiverse students as well as something adults viewed as motivating to practice math and reading skills at home. However, there are many studies that also show that the total volume and time spent with screens is cause for concern because after more than two hours per day, children score lower on thinking and language tests.[2] Some kids also don't learn and retain information from the games because they are too focused on the rewards.

I experienced this directly with one of my sixth-grade clients. His whole conversation revolved around playing video games and earning prizes. One day, he was telling me about a math program called Prodigy. As he was describing the cool characters he wanted to earn, I decided to ask about the math he had to do to get them. He told me he couldn't really remember because he was trying to win his prize. If you don't know that much about gamified learning programs, they are designed to make the content easier or harder depending on how you perform on the questions, so the player keeps earning rewards and stays engaged while making it the "level" at which the individual student succeeds. There is not a clear progression to harder content, so it's difficult to track growth in learning. It's been a few months and I still have no idea what he learned in math this year.

Developmental science acknowledges that kids learn through interactive games and play.[3] While I won't argue with research that shows that video games can be a fun way to engage kids in the learning process, there is no oversight or specific guideline on how educational video games are designed or the way in which they are utilized in the classroom. Some children are more easily addicted to screens than others and, therefore, more vulnerable to the negative impact of screens in school. However, we can generally agree that screens can't replace human interaction or the multisensory experiences that are part of the learning process.

E-Books, E-Textbooks, and Videos

Whenever my daughter has a hard class, she asks me to buy the textbook. Schools have been able to reduce textbook expenses by making them available online. The challenge is that encoding information from reading is a multisensory experience. Encoding is the process by which the brain receives information from the senses about the world, organizes information, attaches meaning, and stores it to use later. The brain relies on multisensory experiences to make sense of the world while building the skills of thinking and reasoning. Book pages are organized sequentially. Even if you can't remember the exact page number where you read something, you know about how far into the book or chapter it is. With an e-book, it's an endless scroll, making it hard to recall where you read a piece of information without rereading sections of the book to find it. A 2023 study showed that comprehension is six to eight times better with physical books than e-readers.[4]

In my daughter's sophomore year of high school, her English teacher asked the class what they disliked most about their freshman English class that they would like to see change. The answer? E-books. They all wanted hardcopies of the books they needed to read to effectively annotate and analyze the content. One exception that I will note is that sometimes, in the case of children with sensory aversions to paper or difficulties managing the volume of information on a page, using screens can be a better way to deliver information because it allows them to compensate for difficulties in another area and access content that they may have otherwise not been able to.

Reading is also increasingly optional. For every article or piece of academic content, there is a video you can watch (or must watch for class credit). This not only increases the time you have to spend on your screen but also the time you spend doing homework in the first place. Audiobooks and read-aloud features increase accessibility for those who struggle with reading but do not provide an opportunity to improve reading skills. AI tools are available to create summaries and outlines of content for studying. You can still find bookstores and libraries, but the practice of sitting around on Sunday reading books and newspapers or playing board games because all the stores are closed is no longer built into the routine of life in many parts of the United States. According to Statista.com, in 2024, 5% of Americans had read more than 12 books in the previous three months while 28.5% had not read any books at all.[5] According to the Dynamic Indicators of Basic Early Literacy Skills (DIBELS) assessments, 54% of first graders were on track for reading in 2023 to 2024, down from 58% in 2019 to 2020.[6] Many adults are not reading books, their children don't see them reading books, and their children are struggling with reading as well.

As information has shifted toward soundbites, video clips, and brief pieces of content, it's easier to choose those information sources over reading longer texts in a fast-paced digital world. Additionally, when people consume large volumes of information in a short period of time, they struggle to retain information long term. Researchers published a study in 2017 that showed that binge-watching reduces the amount of information consolidated into long-term memory.[7] This is consistent with other memory research published as far back as the 1970s that shows that cramming for tests may facilitate recall in the short term but does little to help us retain and recall information over time.[8]

Being able to read and analyze longer and more complex pieces of text as well as retain that knowledge over time is critical for developing expertise in any topic, reading research publications, and expanding critical reasoning skills. Cultivating reading habits in a world overflowing with multi-media is now a conscious effort versus a built-in routine. It is not just the ability to read that is important, it's that reading itself builds focus and attention. Reading stories teaches valuable lessons and social skills. Reading builds vocabulary for self-expression and for writing. It promotes visualization, imagination, and creativity. Helping our children succeed in a digital world full of AI hinges on their ability to gain these uniquely human skills through daily habits and routines.

Assistive Technology

The last thing to note is that assistive technology has become a core part of specialized learning support when a child is struggling with writing, reading, or organization. A common recommendation for kids who struggle with writing and typing is using speech-to-text.

But how many kids and teens do you know who would dare use that technology in the middle of a classroom where their peers could hear them? Scanning in worksheets to edit them on the computer because you are exempt from writing can take five to ten minutes just to set up. By then, the other kids are already halfway down the page and you have fallen behind in your work. Until editable worksheets are readily accessible to students, this is not an efficient option. Sometimes, even if a child completes an assignment, it just never gets uploaded and turned in because there are too many steps to the process. This doesn't seem fair when many kids are already hyper-aware of how much they are struggling. Then the online grading system reminds them they are a failure as their grade drops five percentage points for missing an assignment. Frustration is growing among struggling learners, contributing to anxiety, outbursts in the classroom, and school refusal. These are the learners that find their way to my office.

Having so many tools and activities in one space is also more likely to create distraction, especially for kids with executive function and attention deficits. I know a middle schooler who spends more time figuring out how to get around the controls that are designed to help him focus on the e-text than he spends actually trying to read the passage. Another child I worked with was so focused on the sounds coming from the iPads in the room that he couldn't concentrate on the worksheet he was supposed to be doing with a paraprofessional. For some children with autism, getting time on an iPad is a reward for doing work. Yet children with autism are more vulnerable to the negative effects of screen time including hyperarousal and dysregulation.[9]

There are so many tools available, but it is critical to consider the total balance of technology accommodations, gamified learning programs, video-based learning, and interactive multisensory learning to help children struggling academically become successful and confident learners.

If we want our children to experience academic success, we need more opportunities for learning that provide multisensory, hands-on learning experiences that foster brain growth and development rather than more math and reading games, videos, and assistive technology to compensate for missing skills.

Social Interactions Can Be Reduced to a Video or Emoji

Socially, it is not uncommon to see siblings sitting next to each other, each of them on their own device and minimally interacting with one another. Kids connect with each other on gaming platforms like Roblox but then struggle to navigate social interactions during the school day that require the reading of nonverbal cues and facial expressions.

Many children are pleading for a smartphone in middle school to access the social media platforms where their friends hang out. Without access to the apps, kids feel isolated from their peers and are sometimes left out of social gatherings that were planned through direct messaging and group chats.

Over the years, children migrated from platforms like Facebook to Snapchat and Discord where parents could not see their conversations. These same platforms expose children to bullying, internet trolls, and online predators who are also trying to escape detection by parents or authorities. Privacy protection extends to adults and children alike, putting privacy ahead of safety. The current estimate is that one in five children will be targeted by a predator through online gaming platforms like Roblox and Fortnite.[10] The US child safety agency received over 32 million reports of online enticement, child sexual abuse material, and child sex trafficking in 2022, up 2.7 million from 2021.[11] Various congressional acts and bills have been introduced but as of March 2025, checking the congress.gov website updates reveal that many had not even made it to both the House and the Senate for voting.

Middle school and high school lunchrooms are filled with kids watching videos on social media, messaging friends, and playing video games. If I was a teen today in a new school looking for a friend to have lunch with, the chances of getting eye contact from someone and being invited to sit down are pretty low. If you have social anxieties or insecurities to begin with—not uncommon for anyone at this age—retreating to your phone while eating seems like a great plan, but it's not going to expand your social circle. Common Sense Media reported that the percentage of children watching online videos daily more than doubled from 2015 to 2019. Fifty-six percent of 8- to 12-year-olds and 69% of 13- to 18-year-olds were watching online videos every day, spending on average almost an hour a day.[12]

A term I learned recently is that the way children stay connected to their parents and their friends is through something called "breadcrumbing." They send a video or a funny meme to a person they care about—not specifically to initiate a conversation but to reach out and say, "Hey! Here I am, and I am thinking of you." Now this can backfire if you are sending things like this too much or too often, especially to a crush who is now ghosting you. While it's an attempt to create connection with others, it falls short when there is no response from the person you sent it to or it fails to lead to deeper, more meaningful interactions in person. It is reaching out without the vulnerability that creates trust and security in the knowledge that someone is "there for you." This is where helping your children learn the nuances of social engagement, and how to read social cues becomes exponentially important. To have a friend is to be a friend—not just by exchanging videos or memes but through making time to connect and show others they matter to you. This can only happen with face-to-face opportunities to practice connecting with others and experiencing how initiating social interaction is reciprocated.

As the social world shifts, both parents and children feel like they need to go online to connect with others. Without a foundation of social skills and social awareness combined with knowledge about internet safety, doing this can lead to unintended consequences.

If we want our children to have healthy relationships and social skills, we need to strike a balance between interactions through technology and real-life, face-to-face time spent together without distractions. We also need to teach digital literacy and internet safety, so children can make good choices about who they interact with and in what way.

Everyone Likes Hitting the "Easy Button"

I will admit it. When my alarm goes off on my phone in the morning, I like that I can hit the snooze. I like that I can send someone a text without always getting on the phone when I don't have time to chat but I need to check something off my to-do list or confirm I am coming over for book club. I like that I don't have to spend a lot of time pouring over a map to take a road trip or locate a restaurant. I even like that AI can help me write sales copy—which I am not good at—as a pediatric therapist. It's easy.

But what is easy is also my Achilles' heel at times. If I can send a text, so can everyone else—anytime they want. Then I feel compelled to respond, interrupting my in-person facetime with someone else. If I am too focused on the little blue line on my GPS and I drive somewhere without satellite or smart service, I am completely lost when it stops updating. And, by the way, so are the police officers who haven't learned all the streets of the city they work in. Not exactly comforting if you have an emergency but live in a house surrounded by woods or mountains. If I put a bad prompt into ChatGPT, it spits out five variations of exactly the same information rather than five marketing emails I could actually send out. Time wasted.

Our kids have an even more intense experience. Texts and notifications from social media disrupt them all day once they get a smartphone. They rarely use the "do not disturb" setting and communicate with others in soundbites, not full conversations. Then when those same kids have to volunteer or try to get their first job, they lack the in-person social skills to have polite conversations with customers or maintain their composure when dealing with a difficult customer. Many high schoolers are terrified to call in a food order and talk to a person. They have been trained to use an app not only when ordering from home but also when ordering a meal at McDonalds. But I guess that's fine, right? If we train people to order through an app, then our children don't need to learn customer service if they can just fill orders as their after-school job. (I hope you are detecting the sarcasm in my voice.) The unfortunate reality here is that the current digital world is encouraging children to interact with machines over people, but succeeding in an AI world as an adult requires the human skill of connecting with others for leading teams, collaboration, and problem-solving.

Many children, after experiencing social exchanges in soundbites, struggle to tell cohesive stories in full sentences. Conversations with others often begin with "Let me show you …," as adults willingly follow to see what it is rather than asking them to explain or describe what they experience. In school, older children are using ChatGPT to write essays as they struggle to compose sentences. They try to outsmart the plagiarism software and the "edit tracking" feature in Google Drive by cutting and pasting in small increments and then changing some of the words to make it look more like their own writing. For middle schoolers, we would expect writing to be underdeveloped, so it's a red flag if it seems "too good."

When it came to driving, I purposely had my daughter learn to drive around our city without GPS to learn how the streets connected and alternate routes for getting to school. This has helped her more than once when there has been an accident or roadwork. Even though GPS can be a great tool for finding the fastest route, she also knows what it feels like to type in an address for a restaurant only to find herself 30 minutes away from that restaurant because she didn't double check the city when the location populated in the app. My daughter doesn't know what a road atlas is or how to use it to find her way, so it took her a while to realize that she wasn't even close to her destination. I look at the digital map on the GPS to determine the best route based on what I know about the area. She, like many others in her generation, chooses the fastest time and skips straight to turn-by-turn directions.

What began as the "easy button" for us, adults, has reduced the opportunities for our children to work on social awareness like being respectful of people's time and accepting that sometimes other people are busy. It has limited children's opportunities to practice communicating both verbally and in written form. The mental map that develops when a teen starts driving is optional because GPS is available. When a child isn't good at something, AI makes it easy to find a work-around rather than using perseverance and persistence to develop a skill. The statistic I mentioned earlier about children scoring lower on thinking and language tests after spending an average of just two hours on screens doesn't seem so surprising anymore, does it?

By outsourcing our brains to technology and using technology to make life "easier," we disrupt the multisensory learning process that sets the foundation for children expanding their independence and ability to manage daily tasks.

Cash Is Optional

Contactless payments became very popular during COVID, giving rise to apps such as Venmo, Zelle, and CashApp. It fast-tracked online shopping, and every business needed to upgrade their credit card terminals to include "Tap to Pay." The Apple Wallet makes it possible to tap to pay without even carrying a card. We can easily order online in advance and pick up Starbucks or have UberEats deliver without ever taking money out of a wallet. Services like Netflix and Hulu are provided with automatic monthly transactions to your credit card.

Imagine how this looks to a child. They see adults just holding up their phone to a computer screen and then, like waving a magic wand, they are able to take home all the groceries. They see adults taking coffee off the counter at Starbucks when they didn't even wait in line or hear their parents asking for a "grande vanilla latte." Kids can just turn on the TV and have access to endless content but never see their parents sitting down each month to write checks and pay bills.

Developmentally, children rely on concrete visual cues and modeling to learn how things work. On the surface, it seems like the phone does everything. It seems like you can just take something if you want it because the monetary transaction can be separated from the actual delivery of the product. How do we expect children to know that virtual money they earn when playing video games to buy things is not the same as the money that comes from hours spent at work for a paycheck? Money has become a concept only taught on worksheets at school because children rarely see their parents exchanging cash for purchases. My daughter shared with me that she was the only one at a table of teenagers who knew that you don't leave both a cash tip and write the tip on a credit card receipt. If it wasn't for her, someone's parent's credit card would have been way overcharged—that lucky waiter would have had a 40% tip. These are small things that not everyone thinks about mentioning to their children as they are going through the motions of ordering online and tapping to pay because we, as adults, are focused on the convenience.

There is something different about handing someone a $10 bill or a $20 bill and looking at the singles that they give you back versus doing a contactless payment. It makes you realize that maybe you don't want to pay $7.10 for a "grande caramel macchiato" at Starbucks—especially if you just got that $20 from walking your neighbor's dog. We, as adults, become frustrated when our children don't value money, are constantly asking for things, and expect us to pay for everything.

What is worse is that surveys show that finances are a major stressor for young adults and they don't feel they have the tools to manage money and be financially independent when they graduate.[13] The whole family is frustrated, but it's not intuitive to step back and realize that this evolved in tandem with the rise of subscriptions and contactless payments. Businesses don't want you to watch where your money is going, but they sure do want to make sure they collect it!

As they say, "The road to hell is paved with good intentions." Those small daily transactions add up in ways we never anticipate when the learning could have been happening all along. One of my best friends has a vivid memory as a child watching her grandmother count out the cash rent she collected from tenants as a property owner. Another recounted to me that she watched her grandparents count the money from their butcher shop at the dining room table. I remember being on a $75-a-week grocery budget when my daughter was young—doing the math and putting back anything that wasn't a necessity. These are the money lessons that keep you out of debt or at least make you better able to make decisions about where your money goes. If counting money is just a concept learned in school from worksheets, how can we expect our children to learn skills that will keep them out of debt and allow them to adjust their spending habits to save for a house or support their own children in the future while living in an automated society?

If we want our children to achieve financial independence, they need to see us, their parents, engage with paper money that can be touched, counted, and exchanged outside the classroom while also practicing this skill on their own in real-life situations.

The Internet Never Sleeps and We All Are Running on Empty

The amount of time people spend getting quality sleep and engaging in active movement has also been disrupted. As more and more content becomes internet-based, children and parents alike find themselves doing work and homework online, chatting with friends online, having Zoom calls with Grandma, using computers throughout the day for educational purposes, spending leisure time indoors on video games and binge-watching videos. I am sure even as an adult you have had the experience of looking up from a tablet or phone and realizing that an hour went by in what seemed like ten minutes. We can shop anytime, anywhere. There is no limit to what we can search for or what we can buy. Since many stores incentivize online purchases over ones in the store, consumers are driven more and more to online shopping, and malls are being converted to dorms and activity complexes.

It is not uncommon for both adults and children who wake up in the middle of the night to go on their phone or tablet if it's available. We all have so many reasons to stay sedentary. We can do ten things without ever having to stand up except to use the bathroom and grab some food.

Unfortunately, the blue light coming from screens blocks the production of melatonin, a hormone necessary for falling asleep.[14] Coupled with the constant notifications from apps and restless legs from lack of exercise, it's not a wonder that it's hard to fall asleep at night as your brain runs a mile a minute. Research shows that sleep and exercise are critical to regulating dopamine levels, supporting self-regulation and managing stress.[15] And anyone who has spent any time with young children knows that most of them are in constant motion that only seems to screech to a halt when they have screens in front of them. We, as adults, are fooled into believing they are calm because they are quiet. What is actually going on inside the brain is that high levels of dopamine (the reward-center hormone) are being released with every scroll to a new video, every point rewarded during gaming, and every novel experience on the internet, contributing to overstimulation.[16]

The result? Those massive tantrums that happen with some children when you remove access to a device.

The compounding effect of less sleep and exercise but high levels of dopamine creates the perfect storm for emotional dysregulation. Emotional well-being expands when we learn the habits and routines that set the physiological foundation for self-regulation. It's not just about learning the social nuances of how to engage with others. As parents, we all know that running low on sleep often means running low on patience. Lack of regulating exercise often means low energy and more sedentary time on the couch. Some movement provides energy to the brain and body while other movement promotes calming and relaxation—think roller coaster versus yoga. A need for constant stimulation, entertainment, and quick rewards that is out of balance with movement and downtime makes us feel anxious and uncomfortable when we are denied access to screens. It's the difference between having a regulated dopamine system and one that experiences a roller coaster of highs and lows. Just like any other addiction, adults and children alike experience withdrawal from high levels of dopamine and are affected by this vicious cycle. This cycle creates a consumer that seeks rewards and relief rather than a creator that is focused, regulated, and goal-oriented.

Many adults have the executive function skill of self-control to at least reduce the number of tantrums that they have during the day. Young children don't have a well-developed ability to exercise self-control. If we are all running on empty, it is not a surprise when I hear from school administrators that children are engaging in explosive behaviors that they rarely used to see and getting therapy at earlier and earlier ages for emotional disturbances.

Helping your children have emotional and mental well-being starts with a strong physiological foundation built out of daily habits and routines for balancing screen time, sleep, and movement.

Our Community Is Disconnected in an Overly Connected World

Online, parents and teens can join any group they like with shared interests. While small conversational exchanges are made in Facebook groups and chatrooms, you don't ever have to be fully present. You can have 12 conversations going at once and just scroll back to see what you missed. Because we can participate in events online and in person, there are now too many events to choose from. I expect that a live online course that I am running will never have the number of attendees that signed up to participate. Signing up is now just an expression of interest rather than a calendar commitment, especially if it's free. Participants who did not have a personal interaction with a friend or the speaker don't really feel any sense of responsibility to follow through with their commitment. It's not personal. It feels like just another form and more emails clogging your inbox. It's easy to say, "I will just watch the replay"—even if you never do.

As the pressure and the noise of the digital world grows, there are more things to do than hours in the day. Too many commitments. Too many work deadlines. Too many people sending you emails and text messages to sign up for their courses. In my town, I realized that all the meetings hosted by schools and the board of education seem to be scheduled on Wednesdays. How do you choose between attending a virtual committee meeting, the superintendent's budget meeting, and having dinner with your kids? They are all important, but too many options mean low attendance at most meetings.

This feeling of disconnect from the community is also happening with teens. High school clubs still exist, but most kids don't show up consistently. If they go to a meeting and see a low turnout, they are less likely to go back to that meeting in the future because they didn't connect with anyone. Many marching bands are about half the size they were in the '90s because kids struggle to keep the intense practice schedule, especially if their parents also have signed them up for tennis, math tutoring, and SAT prep classes.

The social behavior and expectations of parents with young children have also shifted. I was talking to a daycare director who has a strict no smartphone policy for her staff. This is to ensure the kids are always being watched and engaged, but parents complain that they aren't receiving pictures and updates throughout the day "like other daycares." Her response? She tells them that she sends out a single update with photos once per day so that she can ensure that the children that attend the daycare get the developmental experiences they need and that the staff's attention is not divided because of time spent on technology. Then she encourages them to make viewing the photos a family event in the evening to create an opportunity for connection and communication. Yet many parents still expect to have direct access to teachers in daycare and private school settings to manage their own anxiety. This just means that kids are getting less attention as teachers struggle to meet the needs and address the concerns of parents. Parents are feeling "connected" to their children through the updates but are failing to connect with their children consistently and in meaningful ways.

Practicing presence is a critical skill. It challenges us to be where we are. It challenges us to follow through with commitments and focus on one meaningful experience at a time. A digital world powered by AI is often just vying for our attention without any awareness of who else may be seeking that attention, even if it is children who desperately want to connect with us, adults.

If we want our children to have healthy relationships and grow up to be confident people with strong personal identities, modeling presence in our interactions with others, giving our children space to connect with other mentoring adults, and practicing presence with them is non-negotiable.

The World Keeps Changing in the Blink of an Eye

Ideas and innovations are being implemented daily in the form of updates to existing apps and web-based platforms. The capabilities of the internet continue to expand across industries. When ChatGPT was released, other AI tools quickly started showing up in search engines, being embedded in Adobe Creative Suites and other design platforms, taking over customer service, and helping us write everything from marketing emails to college essays to legal documents. Just like the iPhone in 2007, AI finally evolved in 2023 to a point that changed the way we do business in the blink of an eye. What follows is a change in the jobs available, work and productivity expectations, and a change in the types of skills our children need to learn to succeed in the digital world as it exists at any moment. That often means that there aren't government policies, research, or existing institutions to help our children learn how to navigate this world. While academia and healthcare will tell you to only use products that are researched-based, innovation always precedes research and the public buys into the marketing that tells us to embrace it. Nutrition labels were only added to food in 1994.[17] What we know about nutrition and how to educate ourselves about what we eat is about 30 years young despite the rise of TV dinners happening in the 1950s. What has happened? A diabetes and obesity epidemic from years of being told processed foods were not harmful.[18] With any innovation, there are inevitably casualties and unintended consequences along the way. As parents and consumers, it then becomes our job to figure out how to navigate it ourselves while simultaneously making the best decisions we can for our children from the information we have available—not wait for Congress to pass legislation to protect our children from what we know many of them have already experienced.

In the current digital world disrupted by the growth in AI, it's not enough to just learn the technology available and how to stay safe online. College students have to know how to harness the power of AI across industries while finding better ways to distinguish themselves with "uniquely human" skills. Current college students say they wish they had more courses to teach them problem-solving, critical thinking, creativity, emotional intelligence, adaptability, and lifelong learning.[19] Unfortunately, as you have learned so far, these are the exact skills that children are struggling with as computer-based learning and screen-based leisure activities have become embedded in daily routines. The educational system of the Industrial Revolution teaches reading, writing, math, science, and history. But is it teaching our children to design and implement solutions to problems—to create and innovate rather than just consume knowledge?

If we want our children to have opportunities in a world where many existing jobs are outsourced to AI, we need to teach them to be adaptive, resilient, lifelong learners.

Rewiring the Brain for Success

As children spend their free time watching video shorts, gaming, social media, and educational content, the way they experience the world shifts away from a sensory-motor perspective. Children spend more time engaging their visual and auditory systems but less time moving, navigating the environment, and engaging in interactive play. The result? The wiring of the brain begins to shift too. Research shows that the brain learns best via multisensory experiences, such as hand-on learning, exploring nature, or dancing and singing to learn new science concepts.[20] Do you remember the song: "the foot bone's...." Engaging all the senses is the optimal way for the brain to create a bank of information from which to operate.

Multisensory learning helps us to connect information infinitely. This allows us to adapt to the world, make sense of our experiences, build on those experiences to refine our understanding of the world, create new things, solve problems, and ultimately create our identity of who we are and what we value. But that learning is disrupted when we do not engage all parts of the brain throughout the day or week in a balanced way. A study begun in 2020 including 11,000-plus children showed significant changes in the brains of 9- and 10-year-olds who engaged with media more than seven hours per day. The MRIs taken revealed "maturation" of the brain that is normally seen in adolescents—a "pruning off" of connections in the cortex of the brain.[21] The brain is always making new connections when exposed to multisensory experiences and novel stimuli. Based on how often we repeat those experiences, the connections in the brain are strengthened—like when learning to walk. This is partly how habits get wired (more on that later). Connections also get "pruned off" when they aren't used—like when we don't use money outside of the classroom—and early "pruning off" isn't desirable. This research suggests we are now seeing more "pruning" than expected at ages 9 and 10 during a period where we would normally see more growth. As a sensory-based therapist, this concerns me.

Information from the world comes in faster than even adult brains can fully process it. I once watched a millennial sitting next to me on a plane toggle back and forth between two phones at lightning speed, going in and out of apps while chatting with friends and collaborating on a work project. It was quite impressive. But knowing that the brain's capacity for storing information is on average seven bits of information at any one time[22] reminds me that there is probably very little chance the millennial will recall everything they did without going back and rereading the details of their texts and emails.

Small opportunities for building brain capacity in the past came in the form of memorizing other people's phone numbers. Pressing the buttons helped provide the tactile and muscle-based sensory feedback to encode those numbers in the brain without having to write them down. Once phone numbers became ten digits, we luckily had the ability to store them in our phones and outsource our limited brain capacity to technology. Now there are very few people who can recall phone numbers of more than five people. There are even fewer children who can remember number sequences greater than two to three digits, yet we still hope that they can learn to easily read four- and five-letter words without sounding them out every time.

I find that I spend a lot of my time in occupational therapy sessions coaching and educating parents on strategies to best support their children through intentional movement activities given their specific sensory and motor profiles. Some children need more speed and spinning while swinging. Others crave the heavy lifting and resistance inherent in climbing and crashing into things or the calming pressure of getting buried under a pile of cushions. When the sensory opportunities are available and there are no screens in sight, the body leans into seeking the sensory inputs it needs to self-regulate.

I want all children to have the best chance possible for happiness and success in life. But if our children's consumption of media is literally changing the wiring in their brains, we have to ask the questions: "Is it for the better? Are my children going to thrive as they get older or struggle to succeed? Is there something that I can do as a parent to make sure that there is a balance between my children's online experiences and multisensory experiences that will help them achieve their true potential?"

These are all the areas that research has shown screen time has impacted children:

- Attention and focus[24]
- Self-regulation and behavior[23]
- Memory[23]

- Social emotional learning[24]
- Vision/visual skills[25]
- Posture and back pain[26]
- Mental health[27]
- Sleep[27]
- Social skill development[28]
- Learning and cognition[29]
- Exposure to online predators and explicit content[30]

If ever there was a time to invest in understanding how children build the skills they need to succeed in an ever-changing digital world, it is now. We can't afford to wait ten years for institutions to adapt their teaching programs to meet the needs of our children or for laws to be passed to protect our children better. There is so much we can do *right now* if we only understand what pillars need to be in place and how to create our own roadmaps to get there. Only then will we cultivate success habits in our children that foster adaptability, resilience, creativity, and problem-solving. And, yes, you can expect to explore and grasp those pillars over the course of this book.

Now that you can see more clearly all the shifts that have happened with the introduction of portable technology and increased screen time, it's tempting to consider a drastic approach to protecting our children through strict screen time limits, but that may be a losing battle when preparing our children to succeed in an AI world. In Chapter 6, we will talk about why.

Turn to Chapter 5 of your Family Playbook to reflect on your family's current media use and some of the changes you could implement before moving on.

CHAPTER 6

Is the Answer Just Limiting Screen Time?

*Time is the only thing we cannot replace,
apart from our health and our lives.
I resent wasting a moment of it.*

—Felix Dennis

I don't think so.

If we look back, many parents raising their kids in the '90s did not have any rules around technology, even though there were studies being done around television. I recall the one piece of advice my mother gave me when I was young: "Don't sit too close to the TV. You will ruin your eyes!" We all know what happened there. TV screens just kept getting bigger and bigger, so we didn't have to sit close. Then smartphones made screens smaller and smaller, straining our eyes even more.

While SMART Boards were invented in 1991, they began showing up in public school classrooms around 2005. The bright lighting of an oversized screen filled the classroom. In 2010, iPads forced children's eyes to focus on smaller fonts and images until they graduated to an even smaller smartphone. The American Academy of Ophthalmology reported in 2024 that the number of people developing nearsightedness in the United States has nearly doubled since 1971.[1] Boston Children's Hospital reports that 20% of children have refractive errors such as nearsightedness, lazy eye, astigmatism, and crossed eyes.[2] Generally speaking, we, as consumers, reasoned that what we gain from using screens far outweighs the sacrifice of our eye health.

As technology continues to evolve, more and more people spend much of their day behind computers for work or glued to their smartphones. We, as adults, value portability to do our work anywhere. We value entertainment. We value connection to others. We value the ability to multitask. We value being able to have knowledge at our fingertips. We spend more time talking about how to manage our stress than we do focusing on managing our overall physical health, never considering that the two might be connected. You might be saying to yourself, "So what? I don't care if I have to wear glasses. No big deal."

You are probably right. But I mention this as a symptom of a bigger elephant in the room. Our desire to save money, get more done in less time, have things that we want when we want them, feel like we belong, get quick wins and rewards, and feel like we are contributing to the world around us in some small way are exactly the things that marketers focus on to get adults to use their products, regardless of the consequences to our health and emotional well-being. It would be naive to think that our children don't share those same core human needs for belonging, significance, novelty, and consistency. Tablets and smartphones can deliver all those feelings with a swipe or a tap. But they can also unlock Pandora's box to a host of long-term consequences—for ourselves, our children, and our world—that we often don't consider in the decisions we make moment to moment as we check our email or pass our children a phone to watch a video while shopping.

Just Because We Get Advice Doesn't Mean We Listen

The American Academy of Pediatrics' 1999 guidelines recommended that "pediatricians should urge parents to avoid television viewing for children under the age of two years." At the time, the media focused primarily on the impact of children in early development given that educational programming on TV was widespread. But that didn't stop media marketing companies from singing the benefits of educational screen time—and parents willingly bought in. In 2006, only 15% of parents reported that their pediatricians discussed media use with them during well visits. By 2007, 90% of parents said their children watched some form of media. This was long before everyone carried around computers in their pockets. Some of the concerns cited from research on media use in children younger than two noted issues like[3]:

- Having the TV on in the background with parent-preferred content reduces parent-child interactions and distracts children from play.
- Reduced interactions and increased distraction interfere with language development, cognitive processing, memory, and reading comprehension.

- Heavy media use in the home affects outdoor playtime and time spent reading.
- Sleep issues can occur when TV is used as a bedtime aid.
- Obesity in preschoolers was associated with media use.

Children from the 2007 study are 20 years old now. The children from the 2011 study are 15 years old now. Many of them are suffering. A 2023 Gallup Poll surveying over 5,000 people published showed that the number of adults diagnosed with depression in their lifetime was 29%, which was 10% more than in 2015 with most of them being between the ages of 18 and 44.[4] In 2023, four in ten (40%) teens felt persistently sad or hopeless according to the CDC's Youth Risk Behavior Survey.[5]

If we step back for a moment, many of us would say that we, as adults, spend a significant portion of the day being sedentary, either working on a screen, socializing on a screen, or binge-watching TV shows … on a screen. While TV may have impacted our childhood development to some degree as far as outdoor playtime, parent-child interactions, and time spent reading, we could not take our devices with us everywhere we went or sit on the couch together, all watching different screens. Social norms around non-screen leisure and educational activities still included using a real camera to take pictures and playing tabletop learning games. The experiences we had as children that cultivated creativity, taught us about managing money, and helped us develop life skills were different from those of children today because there just wasn't an app for any of that yet. However, as adults, we lean into technology to manage our health, our emotions, our stress levels, and our obligations just as our children do.

The idea of limiting screen time as it relates to computers and digital devices continued to evolve somewhere between 2010 and 2014 when the first studies started coming out about the negative effects of screen time, which included more than just television. At that time, our personal computers and video game consoles were still mostly at home. We still shut them down, even in the early 2000s, to go to class, grocery shop, sleep, listen to music, go to sports practice, or read a book. When the iPhone came out in 2007, many stores still closed at 9 p.m. during the week and were closed on Sundays. Yes, there were online marketplaces such as Amazon and eBay in the '90s, but popularity grew exponentially with mobile shopping via apps in 2010. You couldn't carry on a text conversation and exchange videos with someone else when you were eating at a restaurant with friends. You typically had to wait for your favorite song to come on the radio unless you plugged in your iPod to listen to a playlist made from CDs you downloaded into iTunes. Subscriptions to apps like Spotify with endless songs to choose from weren't an option. The industries of e-commerce and social media were still in their infancy. There were physical boundaries at the societal level that kept many of us from engaging with media all day long because technology wasn't as portable and easy to access.

Portable devices were used mainly by Gen Xers and millennials in 2007. Then the iPad was released in 2010. Those of us of the same generation that grew up on cable TV now could pass the joys of channels like PBS and other educational programming to our own children but with a portable device that allowed us to keep engaging with the content we valued simultaneously. At that time, we still didn't really have concerns for ourselves or our children despite the rising publications of books coining terms like "internet addiction" and "gaming addiction."

PBS Kids launched its first augmented reality app for kids in 2011 with help of a Ready to Learn grant from the US Department of Education.[6] It's continued from there as many media companies target parents and sing the benefits of educational games as they find their way into classrooms across the country. Computer games have been marketed as a way to supplement learning while providing "leveled learning" opportunities so that children could practice and progress at their own pace. In some situations, it also provides an easy way for parents to have children practicing reading and math skills at home independently without the need for sitting next to them and doing homework. Convenience and peace of mind that our children are getting what they need for academic development. What else could you want as a parent?

There is only one small issue—they are still struggling to get research that shows that this is the way that kids learn. In fact, most research points to interactive, hands-on, multisensory learning opportunities as showing the best outcomes when it comes to development of life skills and academic success.

It Used to Be Easier to Limit Screen Time

What started as a concern in 1999 around TV screens expanded to encompass portable devices and exposure to screens only intensified for our children. It was easy to limit screen time in 2010 when my child was a preschooler because most kids did not have an iPad. When the SMART Board was installed in her preschool classroom, they scheduled a parent night to discuss all the awesome features of the technology. Meanwhile, the behavior of another child in the class skyrocketed as the visual stressor of the giant, brightly-lit screen in the room was too much for his developing eyes to tolerate.

It took me a while to upgrade from my Nokia and Sidekick phones to a smartphone. We did have an old iPad gifted to us in 2013 with a few games on it. Luckily, at that time, my daughter was not an avid video game player. She was much more interested in practicing gymnastics and playing with her dollhouse by then. In the fourth grade, she received an iPhone due to reasons that were deemed necessary in my family dynamic but not for the purposes of texting friends, joining social media, or downloading gaming apps. These remained off limits. There were not a significant number of children at that time who had phones, so she wasn't missing out. Kids were, however, definitely playing Nintendo and PlayStation any chance they got, but online chatrooms were not commonplace among 7- to 9-year-olds in the pre-Roblox era.

Since all those studies were completed with a focus primarily on television in the home, the findings have been replicated many times over as it relates to device use among parents and children. You will see them cited throughout this book. Studies have expanded to focus on elementary age and teenage children rather than just toddlers and preschoolers.

The American College of Pediatrics published an extensive summary of the research around media use, including smartphones, tablets, and social media in 2020.[7] There are over 113 citations. If you want to read the article, go to this site: https://acpeds.org/position-statements/media-use-and-screen-time-its-impact-on-children-adolescents-and-families. I will highlight just a few of the study findings in this report below:

- A 2017 Common Sense Media report found that 95% of homes have a smartphone and 78% of homes have a tablet, with 42% of children between 0 and 8 years having their own tablet. Toddlers less than two years of age spent an average of 42 minutes each day viewing screen media.

- Most children and adolescents live in homes where there are no parental rules regarding screen time. In one study, less than 30% of children and adolescents 8 to 18 years of age stated there were household rules regarding time spent viewing television. In this same study, 64% of those surveyed stated the television in their homes was left on during meals, and 45% stated the television was left on most of the time.

- A large national sample (40,337) of children 2 to 17 years of age were evaluated in 2016 for their use of all forms of screen time. Those who were exposed to more than one hour per day of screen time had "lower psychological well-being, including less curiosity, lower self-control, more distractibility, more difficulty making friends, less emotional stability, being more difficult to care for, and inability to finish tasks." Those who were 14 to 17 years of age who had more than seven hours a day of screen time were more than twice as likely to have been diagnosed with depression compared to those who only used screens less than one hour a day.

- An online survey of 6,000 children and parents found 54% of children said their parents checked their smartphones too often, and 32% felt they were unimportant when parents were distracted. Over half of the parents said they probably checked their smartphones too frequently, and 28% felt they did not set a good example for their children. In addition, 25% stated they wanted their children to use their smartphones less.

The Tidal Wave of Technology

All this research, yet technology from 1999 to 2024 has only continued to expand and creep into every part of our lives. The fear of tech addiction did not stop the vast majority of Gen Xers from harnessing the power of the internet to make an impact. And then leveraging the power of the smartphone to increase consumer engagement with brands, sell more products 24 hours a day, sell more ad space, and create ways to get labor cheaper and faster.

Adults loved the convenience and the perceived increase in productivity. Working moms and dads could keep working without being confined to the office. But the more kids saw their parents on devices, the more they wanted their own devices too. As households started getting more smartphones, more tablets, more smartwatches, and more laptops, we all could be occupied on screens as a family, doing the things each person is interested in or completing work tasks. Sadly, the tantrums and the battles over using screens or eating dinner and getting ready for bed were not far behind.

Whether it involved adults or children, the message that technology was the wave of the future and our children needed to learn to harness its power resonated with many parents and many school districts. The library was renamed the "media center." Promethean Boards and SMART Boards allowed teachers to access the internet to retrieve information, using school-supported educational sites and media to supplement class lessons. Chromebooks and iPads in schools created opportunities for assistive technology, individualized learning, ways for parents to monitor their children's grades and assignments, and improved data collection around student performance.

At home, we, as adults, love to see our kids playing with their friends online when we can't schedule a playdate. We love to be able to use tracking to know where our children are. We love strategies to keep our children occupied, so we can check off more on our to-do list or talk with friends. We love how easy it is to give our children screen time, so we don't have to deal with typical impatience and toddler meltdowns.

Too bad the research now shows that it just makes it worse. In a 2024 survey of 265 parents, preschool children whose parents relied on "digital pacifiers" struggled to manage their anger and had less self-control.[8] Children who had more difficulty managing anger at the beginning of the study were more likely to have parents who used digital devices for emotional regulation a year later. The study suggests that using devices for emotional regulation disrupts a child's ability to learn important self-regulation skills for later in life. Also, parents whose children had more difficult behaviors relied more on devices for regulation a year later, continuing to disrupt opportunities for building self-regulation skills.

The infiltration of technology continued full force during the COVID pandemic. As we struggled to find solutions to educate our children in quarantine, connect with family and friends, and earn a paycheck, technology was the clear winner. People were not reading research. They were looking for solutions to immediate real-world problems. The initiative to have an iPad or Chromebook for every child became a reality as districts across the country struggled to figure out how to help children access their education during the shutdown. Parents who could work from home suddenly found themselves required to log in and stay glued to their computers or participate in endless Zoom calls during the work day. If you were an essential worker, you may have had to leave your home and your children unsupervised for extended periods of time while they had open access to technology. Google Classroom became a standard, along with other apps that allowed scanning of worksheets and online worksheet completion. Reading and math program subscriptions became more popular as teachers needed a way to monitor a child's reading and math progress from a distance. We got thrown headfirst into a period where, overnight, technology became a must for work and moved to the center of education.

We know now that we want a world where we can get together in person, have teachers that teach us in person in a more interactive way, and go to the playground whenever we want. But the way that phones, tablets, and laptops have embedded themselves into our every life experience did not go away. Chromebooks are standard issue. There are very few payphones anymore, so having your own phone is a must. You are a social outcast in middle school and high school without a phone or some sort of access to chatting via online gaming.

Stop Trying to Limit Screen Time

What I am trying to say is—you have an impossible task of parenting and effectively limiting screen time in a world that is shifting as many interactions as possible to online platforms. Heck—malls are dying and stores are going bankrupt because people shop more online for better prices than in person. It probably seems like the world is against you. As much as parents "know" they should be monitoring screen time, it's a bit like evening TV in the '90s—it is almost always on. As online access to the world and all its opportunities increased, the physical boundaries around screen use started to fade. We finally started talking about limiting screen time enough that Apple heard the cry of people looking for how to set limits on screen time for their children having meltdowns and tantrums around technology, but the response was weak at best.

Can you set a time limit on apps? Sure. Can you also hit the "ignore" button or ask for more time? Absolutely. You can pay for subscriptions that will impose time limits for children on their devices too. If COVID taught us anything though, it is that apps and AI can never be a substitute for teaching skills for how to manage time, learn positive social interaction skills, and replace face-to-face contact. That includes outsourcing an opportunity to collaborate with your children and empowering them to be in control of managing their device use versus the device managing them.

The makers of apps and websites track one thing: engagement. How long do you stay on a site? How many times do you click and interact with content? How many times do you go back to the site? How good are they at grabbing and keeping you focused on what they want you to focus on? Remember, they are in the business of selling their apps. You and your children's usage is how they improve their technology to make it increasingly addictive. They are not thinking of the health and well-being of children. They are not thinking about "balancing screen time with the rest of the skills of life." Their goal is to profit from their product with as many users as possible who either have a subscription or entice paid advertisers to place ads on their sites. That's it. It doesn't get simpler than that. If you work for a company that sells something, this might sound familiar, but you probably don't want your child to be the consumer being sold to.

Is "limiting screen time" the best answer we have? Absolutely not. We, as parents, are basically setting ourselves up for a battle of wills unless we work smarter, not harder. We do this by understanding how the brain and body work. This guides the habits and interaction strategies necessary to help children become the best versions of themselves in a world where technology wires them for distraction, disorganization, and even addiction. (Expect to find more information and guidance on this in Part 2.)

What Are the Current Guidelines?

The current American Academy of Pediatrics (AAP) recommendations for healthy media use habits are as follows[9]:

- **Babies under 18 months:** If you do introduce digital media, make sure it's high quality and avoid solo media use.

- **Children ages 2 to 5:** One hour or less of screen time per day. Parents should co-view media with children to help them understand what they are seeing and apply it to the world around them. Choose interactive, nonviolent, educational, and prosocial media. Find other activities to do that are healthy for their bodies and minds.

- **Children 5 years and older:** Make sure media use is not displacing other important activities such as sleep, family time, and exercise. Check their media use for health and safety.

- **Tweens and Teens**: Engage teens in conversations about media use, digital citizenship, what they see and read, who they are communicating with, and what they have learned.

The AAP took it a step further in 2024 to create the "5 Cs of Media Guidance."[10] These include considering (1) child, (2) content, (3) calm, (4) crowding out, and (5) communication. Check out healthychildren.org to learn more.

Rising awareness among lawmakers about the negative impact of social media on mental health in teens and the impact on availability for learning in the classroom has prompted both state and local governments to reconsider the value of implementing guidelines for schools regarding cell phone policies. There is now so much guidance out there at the academic level, it's overwhelming. It's not an action plan, and it's not a hard boundary that limits people's choices. It's considerations. I don't know about you, but I subscribe to the mantra that "failure to plan is a plan to fail." For me, this guidance is good for raising awareness but easy not to implement, just like the guidance in 1999.

While tech giants like Meta, Amazon, Apple, and Google are experts at engagement and growing their consumer base, many of the founders of these companies and people who work in Silicon Valley do not embrace technology when it comes to their children. Instead, they send them to Steiner Waldorf Schools where there is no technology in the classroom before age 12.[11] Steve Jobs admitted when the iPad was released that his children hadn't used it because he restricted screen use in his home. Former Facebook executive Chamath Palihapitiya told an audience at Stanford, when discussing social media, that his children "aren't allowed to use that shit."[12] Jeff Bezos attended a Montessori preschool, as did Larry Page and Sergey Brin, the founders of Google. Jeff Bezos is now partnering with local organizations to open Bezos Academy preschools in multiple states, using a Montessori-inspired curriculum.[13] It seems that the architects of search engines, social media, online shopping, and portable technology benefited from having been afforded a multisensory approach to learning in their youth to become leaders and creators. Now they are passing that opportunity on to their own children, steering them away from the very technology that is being sold to schools as an educational solution and to parents as a means of social connection.

Time's Up!

Since the last thing the businesses of the world want is for you and your children to reduce use of technology, I am going to give you some simple first steps to help you succeed with limit-setting around screens regardless of how much your family currently uses screens each day.

First, remember how rewarding and stimulating screen time is for the human brain and how hard designers work to engage consumers. But there is another reason it's hard for children to put down their devices. The brain is not wired to pay attention to time as an indicator of when to stop a task. The brain is wired for task completion. One of the challenges for people with obsessive compulsive tendencies is that the brain does not feel a sense of completion with certain tasks.[14] So they repeat things compulsively to manage their anxiety around the feeling of incompletion and/or that something bad will happen if they don't engage in the compulsion. If your child came up to you and grabbed your phone out of your hand in the middle of a text message, you would probably throw a fit. Why? You might say it's because you're grown up and your child is being disrespectful. Maybe. After all, you have reasons to be on your phone, right? Or you are triggered for the exact same reason they have a meltdown when you stop the video game mid-play: the task got disrupted, and the brain didn't know what to do, so it triggered a fight-flight response. Knowing this, you are now ready to change your strategy and set your child up for success.

Seven Steps to Help Your Children Put Down Their Devices

1. **Set a VISUAL timer** for about five minutes before screen time ends. You are still choosing when and how often you give your child a device. A visual timer is important as it's much easier to see if there is "a lot" or "a little" time left when making a judgment on starting a new game or video. Plus, if it's set for five minutes before, they have time to finish a video even if the timer goes off to have a sense of completion.

2. **Teach MONITORING.** Teach your child that if a video or a level ends, they should check the timer to keep track of how much time is left, so they can choose a shorter or longer video to watch with your approval.

    Many of the children that I work with thrive on using a visual timer since the passing of time is very hard to judge when you are having fun: "Time flies." It's the same when you are doing something you hate: "A minute feels like an eternity." Remember that we "feel" time even though it's a measurable number of minutes in a day that never changes. It is something concrete that we have created for something that was never meant to be concrete, and then we wonder why our kids start parroting back to us, "Five more minutes," when it's time to go. Five more minutes were up ten minutes ago.

3. **Create SHARED CONTROL.** Go over to your child when the timer goes off, and check to see how close the video or game level is to being completed. If your child has chosen something that continues beyond five minutes (which is pretty rare these days), then have them choose a stopping point, and you be in control of the "stop/pause button."

4. **Collaborate with your child FIRST.** There will be children who refuse, can't stop, or immediately click the next thing. If this is your child, you might need to set a boundary. Give a reminder that either they need to give you the device when the video/game level ends or you will need to take the device. Share with them the consequence for their choice while also setting them up for success. Decide in advance what the next activity will be so that there is something for your child to transition *to*, not just *away from*.

5. **Determine CONSEQUENCES.** As a parent, it is your decision to determine any consequences thereafter, such as limiting access to a device for a certain period of time or reducing the number of minutes your child gets to use a device the next time. Either way, communication is key. Do not assume failure. Always let your child know what the consequences are for making a choice that isn't within the family use guidelines. Then follow through. While you may be inclined to give second and third chances or get caught in a negotiation, remind yourself that children thrive on

consistency and predictability. Following through with a consequence builds trust and mutual respect.

6. **PRAISE good choices.** Make sure to always give your child credit for following your guidelines around use to build an environment of collaboration, positive feedback, and mutual respect.

7. **RINSE AND REPEAT.** Consistency is key. It will take time to build this habit, but when a child sees you responding calmly and consistently with boundaries and expectations, it helps them regulate their own emotions as well.

A word to the wise: Don't get caught up in emotions and a battle of wills where there will always be a clear loser. Someone will walk away crying, and it's either you or your child. Everyone will be stressed. But when you connect and collaborate, you foster an environment of mutual respect and become your child's guide to learning skills to succeed in a digital world.

You Are Probably Saying, "I Wish It Were That Easy!"

We try to do right by our children by limiting screen time because the experts have told us that too much is not good for a young child's development. In fact, the research shows that it is actually common for parents to report that they do limit the amount of time their children spend in front of a screen at younger ages.[15] But there is also what we might call … creep. A few minutes watching a video on the way to soccer practice. Another video while in the cart at the grocery store. Playing a game while waiting for food at a restaurant. It's an easy thing to use to help your child "behave" in public or be quiet, so you can focus on driving. In the rush out the door, parents don't often think about bringing a "busy bag" of non-screen activity options. Most of us don't count "creep" toward the total minutes of screen time during the day (at least until we see the weekly screen time report pop up on our phones).

It's not surprising that, as parents, we all handle our screen time decisions in accordance with our family's lifestyle. As a working mom, my daughter was pretty much either at school or in after-school programs where there was not yet a lot of technology present during playtime or downtime. In the evenings, I admit she did occasionally play some games on the tablet while I made dinner, but I am a 30-minute meal kind of gal, so that didn't yet qualify as "too much screen time." Regardless of if you experience creep a little or a lot, packing a "busy bag" is a great on-the-go option for reducing screen time opportunities.

If Your Child Is Neurodiverse

As a pediatric occupational therapist, I know so many children that don't have play skills and struggle to do homework independently. Children with learning disabilities, developmental delays, speech delays, and diagnoses such as ADHD and autism spectrum disorder (ASD) struggle to entertain themselves, expand on their play skills, and socialize with their peers. These kids are at a higher risk for developing an unhealthy relationship with technology because it's "done for you," doesn't require a lot of motor or social skills, and is highly reinforcing. Many of you may have at least one child who falls in this category and is struggling with screen time. As a parent, it's also more challenging to raise children with diverse needs because it does take more effort, time, patience, and advocacy. Parents need a break. Social interaction can be a struggle. Playing on the iPad may be the only time of day that a child sits down so mom or dad can take a shower.

There was a study done about parent-child interaction for children with autism spectrum disorder (ASD). It showed that screen time was much more prevalent for both the parent and the child in the household.[16] It's okay that, as a parent, you may be looking for a little relief or a little interaction with other parents like you for support. Kids are naturally drawn to the lights and high reinforcement that technology provides while it helps them to "block out" the world around them. But, as you have likely guessed, there's a downside to this. Another study showed that unrestricted access to video games, especially if not regularly monitored by parents, predicted aggression in boys with ASD.[17]

I had a child client once who was obsessed with Disney movies. When he went through a period where his movie watching was higher than usual, his behavioral team was able to correlate that with his screen use. They put a plan in to rebalance the time he spent watching Disney and the time where he was supported in engaging in more active play. This only happened when his team started looking at screen time as a possible reason for his behavior.

It's challenging when your child is nonverbal and doesn't "play" like other kids. You can't say, "Go find something to do while I make dinner." You always have to know where your child is. You always have to make sure your child is not opening drawers and cabinets that are either unsafe or will leave you with a big mess to clean up. For parents who face this every day, I commend and applaud you for your ability to show up, day in and day out, even when sometimes both you and your child are running on three to four hours of sleep. If your child has a disability, talk with therapy providers and school staff about how much screens will or will not be used as a reward for your child. Working with your support team to increase the time your child spends in goal-directed movement and play activities while finding alternative rewards and learning strategies is an important piece of the puzzle as you try to manage their screen time beyond the use of a visual timer. This is something we'll revisit in greater detail later in the book.

Remember: Replacing Is Reducing

The decisions a parent of a neurotypical child would make on how best to balance screen use with facilitating engagement with other activities will likely be very different from a parent who has a child with a learning disability or a parent who has a child who is a gifted athlete. The key thing to remember is to be mindful each day of creating opportunities for non-screen activities that cultivate uniquely human skills. Help your children build skills for engaging with a world that is often overwhelming and overstimulating one activity at a time.

Intentionally taking back the way we are raising our children with a better understanding of what a child needs to develop into a leader or creator might be the only way we can rebalance the scales. Right now, the internet is raising our children. The good news is that there is quite a lot of research and guidance around habits that the brain and body need to develop. So let's stop focusing on the PSA of limiting screen time and start focusing on what we are adding to the daily experiences of our children so they can thrive in an AI world. Doing this gradually resets the boundaries that slowly disappeared into the black hole of the internet. This will help both you and your children be more present, develop connections with others, expand creativity, regulate emotions, and build uniquely human skills for the job of living. I know you want the best for your children. No one has the exact answer for every child about what that is, but I promise you that it is possible—armed with the knowledge and strategies I give you in Part 2—to create an action plan that fits your family and aligns with your values.

> You have made it to the end of Part 1. Once you have completed this, let's shift to Part 2: The Five Pillars and Your Personal Plan.

Part 2

The Five Pillars and Your Personal Plan

While some of us would like to cling to a five-step protocol or find ourselves saying, "Just tell me what to do," most of us will also admit that, long term, we like to make our own decisions and our own plans based on what works for us. Personally, I always like to start with a roadmap, but I forgive myself when I find myself forging my own path, taking some strategies, and leaving the rest. HIIT workouts are great … if you don't have knee and back injuries. Eating eggs is good for you … if you don't have a food allergy. The point is this—in order to make long-term and sustainable changes, you have to be invested in a plan that is realistic for you and your family, and be able to see the results for yourself.

That is why I am giving you Five Pillars of success—*not* five steps—and a Family Playbook that you customize to your family. Each pillar presented in Part 2 will give you an opportunity to reflect on current habits and the areas of your family's life where you can consider how to rebalance screen time with multisensory life experiences. These experiences should create space and opportunities for your children to develop physically, emotionally, intellectually, and spiritually. Don't worry, I will make sure that you also understand the "why" behind the strategies and suggestions, so you can decide how to customize your plan.

Completing the Family Playbook as you read will make it easy to create a customized plan, so you can parent more intentionally in this digital and AI-driven world. If you have made it this far and haven't yet accessed that playbook, pause and take a moment to do that here: aubreyschmalle.com/uniquely-human-playbook.

Up next is the first pillar: Save yourself first. You will definitely want to start taking notes.

CHAPTER 7

Pillar 1: Save Yourself First

*Parent Goal: Your children will develop
healthy relationships and social skills.*

Solution: Cultivate them in your own life first.

When your head is spinning, processing emails, sending text messages, checking social media, signing up for fall sports, etc., it's easy to focus on the to-do list even as your child may be calling your name. However, from the child's perspective, all they see is that the phone must be more important than they are, so they eventually start asking for the phone instead of asking for you. We can continue to not be present and disconnect from our children if we give them something to connect to, like a device. As a parent of a younger child, it's easy to see what your child is doing on the tablet since they are usually watching some sort of video or playing an educational game. For a teen that is texting friends, watching Reels on Instagram, and doing homework all at once, it's a little harder to tell. It's easy to get frustrated when we see their heads constantly looking down at their phone while the world passes by. However, when we step back from that moment, we could argue that what we see is a reflection of ourselves (except, of course, we have much more self-control and have better reasons for being on our phones).

We are all doing the dance as parents. We are pulled in more directions than ever before. Most of us don't have personal assistants checking and filtering our email or handling our text messages. Most of us don't have a team deleting the spam out of our inbox or registering our children for summer camp as soon as it opens so we can get a slot. We are human and we can only do so much. Every day we make a choice of the things we want to prioritize. If your child is hurt, work, all of a sudden, becomes significantly less important. Some of us never miss a workout. Some of us never miss a school performance. Some of us go to every Sunday family dinner. Some of us work so hard there isn't room for anything else. Some of us just … don't. This is not to judge anyone's decisions about how they spend their time. I don't know your circumstances, but I do know that the first step in making a change in any aspect of your life is to decide. Decide that your children's success and happiness are a major priority. Decide to commit to saving yourself first before it becomes an emergency and you don't have a choice. The results of that decision will pay dividends as you seek to guide your children toward lives of success as well.

The disconnect between parents and kids plays out in intact families, families with abundant financial resources, single-parent households, and low-income families alike, even if the circumstances in each household differ. The common factor is that devices are everywhere and the world we live in now is "on demand." As parents, we have a responsibility to model, mentor, and monitor our children's behavior.

Then guide them on how to master the power of technology without getting swallowed up by the dangers that lurk within. As parents who want our children to succeed in all areas of life, it is critical to put the foundation and habits in place that help our children grow into leaders and creators, not the consumers that Big Tech would like them to be. If we lean into technology rather than a Montessori-esque, multisensory approach to growth and development, we may be inadvertently setting our kids up to compete with AI rather than navigate the changing tide of the Information Age.

Model Success Habits

When my daughter was 5 and 6 years old, her caregiver, as I mentioned, played Candy Crush frequently. This game became really popular among women ages 35 and older. In an article written in 2019, a representative of Candy Crush said that of the 270 million users, 9.2 million play for three or more hours per day with the average user playing 38 minutes per day.[1] Gaming has become a normal part of our culture. Research shows that 48% of gamers are women, and the average player is 35 years old.[2] I find that statistic completely mind-blowing because all of the attention to gaming is mostly on fathers and children.

As moms, many of us aren't out playing Fortnite, Call of Duty, or Minecraft, but that doesn't mean we aren't gaming on our phones. I have a very distinct memory as a child of my mother getting hooked on playing Zelda on the original Nintendo console. She played for hours. When she beat it, she put it down and her "gaming addiction" was over. But I remember it because I remember how disconnected I felt from her while she was gaming and how her normal *mom stuff* fell by the wayside. It happens even when we don't realize it or think it's a problem.

Of the 3.24 billion people that play video games, 2.6 billion play mobile games using their smartphones.[3] These statistics don't encompass use of social media or the amount of time that adults spend on the computer registering their children for activities, looking for things to do around town, answering work emails, or tracking their fitness levels and spending habits. Rather than give you an excessive amount of research and statistics, I will get straight to the point. As we start to consider the success habits we want to instill in our children, it's important to take stock of where we spend our time throughout the day, how our children see us engaging with technology, and what subtle or not-so-subtle cues we are giving them. Are we teaching them through our actions that screens are valuable to fill time, stay entertained, connect with others not in our immediate space, and find information? Are we teaching them that these things are more valuable than being present with the people we are sharing an experience with, or are we teaching them that it's important to always be seeking a balance between time spent on technology and time spent connecting with the sensational multisensory world around us?

I recently came across a mom who made an Instagram account: @brookeraybould. She shared how she used to spend a lot of time following mommy blogger content and commiserating with parents about the hardships of raising children. There was a lot of complaining, but it never helped her be a better mom, so she changed the "radio station" and started engaging with positive, enriching content. When this mom started listening to motivational content from successful entrepreneurs, athletes, and other high performers, it led to her implementing habits of success in her own life and speaking the language of success to her children. She was happier and so were her kids.

I can attest to having the exact same experience in my own life. At one point, I was in a place where it seemed like the world was against me. There was no choice but to start making changes. First it was changing the "radio station," so I could change the voices in my head that told me I couldn't. Then it was figuring out how to implement the habits that reflected my new mindset—one habit at a time. Exercise is now a regular part of my week. I allow myself to take vacation time without worrying that my business will collapse. I internalized that as a single mom, there is no shame in accepting help when you need it. I developed a love for gardening that gets me doing something physical and learning something new regularly. I use my phone to research gardening information and listen to inspiring podcasts, but then I get up and take action.

While my journey is far from over, it was the best thing I could have done for my child because my growth gave her space to grow as well. The advice I gave her matched my actions, and she began adopting those same mindsets and habits through her teen years—the time when many kids struggle emotionally to figure out their identities and pull away from their parents. Of course, as a teen she hated when she heard herself repeating words she heard from me—to be expected—but she loves the life she is building for herself and the opportunities that come her way because of it. While I certainly can't take all the credit for that, I know that not changing would have made it very easy for her to look for other, potentially less-than-ideal, role models to shape her identity.

Many parents I meet are hesitant to discuss their own screen use but ask me questions about how to get their children off screens. I offer a few suggestions but mostly rely on modeling different behavior and explaining how they can support their children outside the session with the engagement strategies I am using. During my sessions, the kids will ask me to play theme music for their obstacle courses, which unfortunately requires that I search YouTube quickly because I usually don't have the proposed theme music readily available in CD form. As I search up "Indiana Jones Theme Song" quickly, I find a child rushing to my side to watch the video associated with it. I make a point of saying, "The gym is not for watching videos. I am just looking for music." And then I place the phone on the counter, screen side down and walk away from it. My visual timer keeps me from having to touch my phone during the session, so I can be fully present. If the parents are in the room, I hope that they see this process. If they are trying to grab a moment to catch up on work during the session, either their children or I will call out to them, "Hey, watch this!" Then we wait patiently at the starting point of the course for mom or dad to pick up their head and cheer them on. If that's not working, then I invite the parents to have a "job" in the session that requires two hands and limits their ability to check their phone. Some parents have persistent children who rush over the second the phone comes out of their parent's pocket. They quickly put it away because they realize their children won't play with me if they don't.

Cell phone dynamics play out between parents and children all day long. My hope is that by creating space for connection and engaging parents actively in their children's play and exploration process, they too will learn the skills to be present and engage with their children outside the session, celebrating their wins and modeling presence.

CHAPTER 7

Stop Letting Others Push Your Boundaries

Boundaries are essential if you are going to start living intentionally and modeling success habits for your children. Often when we hear about people setting boundaries, we think of it in terms of intimate relationships with partners or family members, but setting boundaries actually starts in small ways too. Physical boundaries are actually the easiest place to start.

Remember when cubicles were common for office culture? The idea was that if there were walls between people, they would focus more. Of course, that didn't turn out as intended because people just peeked around the partitions to connect with their coworkers. Now with open concept office spaces, people have to filter out distractions around them, but many still socialize by sending messages in shared documents on the computer when they can't send text messages. People will always find ways to connect with each other. Technology has made that possible by removing all the physical barriers.

I had the same experience when my office was positioned too close to the waiting room. When kids arrived, they saw my office door was open and ran right in to greet me and ask me to play. No closed door meant I was available, right? Never mind that they were 15 minutes early for their therapy session and I was trying to finish a report. So I moved my office away from the waiting room and added a door. Did it stop every child from rushing in? No. But it was a prompt for parents to encourage their children to wait patiently until I came to get them.

There are so many ways for us to connect with others via email, social media, messaging, and virtual meetings. It almost feels like we have no excuse not to answer someone immediately who wants to get in touch with us, but when we accept that logic, we set ourselves up for distraction and overwhelm.

Many of us sat at the dinner table with our parents telling us to make sure that our friends knew not to call during that time. Telemarketers purposely violated that boundary, knowing families were at home, but many parents exercised the option not to answer—especially after answering machines were invented. Now, every app has an automated notification option a thousand times worse than the dinner hour telemarketers.

Many of us, adults, justify keeping our phone within arm's reach "in case there is an emergency." We invest in smart watches to make it even easier to keep in touch with family members and friends as we coordinate gatherings or talk about the day's events. We don't want to unplug, but it is necessary.

For myself, I made two important physical boundary shifts that changed my ability to be more present and show up better as a parent.

Physical Boundary 1: I set up "do not disturb" on my phone; however, I designated certain people to be allowed to come through for emergency purposes and apps that I flagged as "safe" to deliver notifications to run my business. Everything else I can check when it's convenient for me.

This gives me the mental space to be more present with my clients with less distractions around administrative tasks, but it also improves my stress level as I'm not compelled to constantly check my phone because it "might be important." I have fewer decisions to make, which means more mental space to think clearly and pace myself during the day. Also, I applied this to when I'm making dinner and spending quality time with my daughter talking about her day.

Physical Boundary 2: When I make time to spend with my child—like watching a movie, playing a game, or working on a project—I put my phone down and ask that she do the same. Sometimes playing some music in the background helps reduce the desire to check our phones because we are getting mental stimulation from the music as well as the activity.

Being present without trying to take pictures and getting distracted by seeing missed notifications has helped us to protect our quality time and leave space for important conversations or even just playing with our dog. He puts himself in charge of family time by alternating who he brings his toy to while playing fetch.

The two physical boundaries aren't perfect, but they are intentional. When I get off track, I can take stock and recalibrate. If I can declutter my own mind from the constant pull of the apps on my smartphone, it gives me more patience and more capacity to parent intentionally. Then I can expand the phone-free expectation to my entire household during family time. Physiologically, reducing the number of tech disruptions positively impacts cortisol levels (stress hormones) that rise in response to digital stress and information overload.[4] Just shifting from being reactive to being intentional can have a major impact on overall stress which gives us, as parents, greater capacity to be patient with our children.

If you choose to do these things too, tell others (including your family) that this is your plan, explain why you're doing it, and explain that if they don't hear from you right away, they can assume that you might be busy. This way you can also head off the inevitable, "Why didn't you respond to my text?"

Setting up these boundaries will be challenging at first. No one likes change, and I guarantee you will get comments from those around you who may be used to you responding and engaging with them immediately. Even your favorite mobile game will kick it into high gear by offering you rewards and creating urgency to play so you don't lose points or go down a level. Be prepared, and hold your boundary. To save your sanity, turn off the notifications for apps that are relentless.

Maybe You Need to Switch to a Flip Phone

For some of us, we are so used to being able to access content on our phones all day long that we not only need to set boundaries with others, we need to do something more drastic to set boundaries with ourselves.

I recently came across a story shared by a dad on Instagram who, with his wife, decided to switch to using flip phones. Here is what he had to say:

- His memory improved because he couldn't just look things up all the time. He had to remember key things throughout the day, like directions and appointment times. With less noise from his phone, it was actually possible.

- They explored the community more and connected with more people because they spent more time going on outings to learn about the world around them instead of looking everything up in advance on their phones.

- Their children did not see them constantly engaging with a screen. As a result, their children's screen time naturally decreased.

- The lack of connectedness online was a good thing. They texted less because it was inconvenient on a flip phone, and they sought out direct face-to-face contact with others or deeper phone conversations. This led to more meaningful connections with others rather than just a high volume of connections.

Each of these shifts are exactly the changes we hope to foster in our children so that they feel more competent in life skills, have more meaningful and fulfilling relationships, and experience academic success. There are many phone options out there for kids that allow you to stay connected to them for emergencies but that don't have internet and social media. Existing federal communication policies use age 13 as the cut-off point for data sharing permissions for children,[5] but that age is not based on developmental readiness. Johnathan Haidt, author of *The Anxious Generation*, recommends that children not have social media accounts before the age of 16. If you are concerned about your children's developmental readiness as they approach the teen years, now is the perfect time to explore cheaper alternatives to a smartphone for you and your children.

Disconnect to Reconnect

Helping children develop social skills, mental health, and positive behaviors requires a fundamental shift in the way we approach the world on a day-to-day basis. For many of us, the pull to connect to content, send a text message, or reach out to others on the internet via social media has overtaken the pull to be present in the spaces we find ourselves within the community. But what is the impact of that on our ability to connect with others? How does it impact our ability to connect with ourselves, self-reflect, and manage difficult emotions? How is it disrupting opportunities to make observations about our world and others' behaviors so that we gain perspective? What are we communicating to others when we are constantly looking down at our phones to "pass the time" instead of taking in the experience that is right in front of us?

I was at a coffee shop today, waiting for my order but not looking at my phone. I was just taking in the busyness of the cafe. Almost every table was filled with people doing work, meeting up with friends, tutoring math concepts, or just taking a moment away from the world to have a cup of coffee free of distraction. I have always loved people-watching. I think about how everyone is interconnected, but we can all be in the same coffee shop, leading completely different lives. Sometimes seemingly disconnected people have a shared experience, like when a fire alarm goes off or a "Karen" walks into the shop and completely disrupts the experience of the others having coffee dates, focusing on work, or studying. These thoughts only really occur to me when I take a moment to be present in the space that I am in, recognizing that I am part of a larger community made up of many individuals and being open to the possibility that I could make a connection with someone at the coffee shop who may shape the course of my life for the better.

As I waited for my order and watched the woman in front of me get her order filled, she picked up her coffee and pastry, smiled at me, and went on her way. Just a smile. But we often forget how important smiles are to helping others connect with us or bringing a glimmer of happiness to an otherwise sad day. With our heads down, looking at our phones, we communicate that we are not approachable. We communicate a lack of interest in connecting with others. We send a message of "I am busy, don't bother me." Sometimes we really are intentionally avoiding interacting with others. My teenage clients have shared that they wear headphones or look at their phones to intentionally deter spontaneous social interactions with strangers because it's too overwhelming for them. Others do all these things out of a cultivated habit to just keep filling the time or because they are succumbing to the compulsion to check their phones.

From a parenting perspective, if you are constantly looking at your phone while trying to give your children instructions or saying, "Go get ready for bed," how likely is it that your children will listen? Is it likely that your children will easily stop doing something they prefer to be doing, like playing Legos, and shift instead to what you are asking? Not very.

Why is this?

The answer is connection and shared intention. Developmentally, children crave connection with their family and spending quality time with them. As children move into the middle years, this shifts toward craving connection and belonging with their peers. In high school, this expands further into connecting with the larger community as they continue to grow their autonomy and independence: being part of a sports team, having a summer job, exploring places to go to college, volunteering, etc. All of this comes after the foundation of feeling safe within themselves and connected to their family. It goes without saying that many children who grow up in broken homes never experience this sense of connection and safety. In some families, children experience connection to each other but not to their parents. In other families, children are connected to one parent but not the other.

Sadly, the most vulnerable children are also the most impacted by living in a world where connecting with others and building a sense of belonging is disrupted by the presence of hand-held devices. Many children don't feel that the adults they care about are approachable or want to connect with them because there is always a device between them. The message that "you are not as important as what is happening on my phone/tablet/computer" gets sent loud and clear over and over on a daily basis. It's not surprising that what often follows is tantrums, "not listening," and attention-seeking behaviors obscuring their cries for connection and love. Being aware of this as a parent—and being very intentional with when and where you use a device—can help you foster a relationship with your children where they feel noticed and loved. When you follow "let's go get ready for bed" with setting down the phone and going with your children upstairs so everyone can get into their pajamas, connection and shared intention are cultivated.

Make Sure Your Children Feel Seen

Opportunities for connection and shared intention provide long-term support for children's mental and emotional well-being—the foundation for helping them move to that next developmental stage of belonging with peers. Children develop confidence in themselves and their abilities when given a strong family foundation to face inevitable adversity in a world where everyone does not have the same shared values. If we want our children to have healthy relationships and grow up to be confident people with strong personal identities, modeling presence in our interactions with others and practicing presence with them is non-negotiable.

Kids want to be with you. They want to feel seen, and they want to feel loved. They want to know that they matter. This is an innate need born into every human—a basic human need that is often disrupted by the presence of screens embedded in human interactions that changes the priorities and daily experiences of life. We, as adults, need to get more done in less time. We forget to smile. We forget to connect. We forget that sometimes things need to take longer for the greater good of our children. It's not that parents don't seek out opportunities they think will help their children develop social skills and learn. They do. But they also have been marketed to by the internet and pressured from other parents who have received the same message to think that involves signing up and paying for someone else to build these skills.

The reality is, somewhere in there, we have to ask ourselves, "What is the balance?" Yes, activities are important. Yes, our bosses expect us to get our work done. Yes, we need to create space and opportunities to connect with our children. Every family figures out how to achieve that balance in a different way. But we can never forget that meeting the human needs outlined in Tony Robbins' 6 Human Needs framework like certainty in routines and unconditional love, opportunities for novel exploration, and connection to others set the foundation for health, wellness, and happiness for adults and children alike.[6]

Once you start making small changes and practicing presence, it's easy to start parenting more intentionally. This is where adding books, podcasts, and YouTube videos from high performers can be helpful in shifting your mindset, so you can begin shifting the mindset of your children. Interestingly, I haven't really found many parenting blogs or videos that have done as much for developing my leadership skills as a parent as compared to what the content from high performers delivers. Do I still need strategies at times on how to communicate effectively with my child and how to respect and empower my child to find her own identity? Definitely. Communication is a skill that is cultivated, especially with kids. We will cover this more in depth in another chapter. For now, just focus on saving yourself first.

Success Habits to Model for Your Children

- Take more opportunities to *not* check your phone.

- Trade in your smartphone for another device.

- Be present on outings. Take in the world around you, and begin to notice those who aren't. See them in a different light, and become more aware of a connected world that is, in reality, very disconnected.

- Take time to smile and make someone else's day, whether it's your children or a total stranger in a coffee shop.

- Identify days and times throughout the week when you can slow down. This may mean doing less and not overscheduling activities, having fewer social commitments, or putting your phone on "do not disturb" while you are making dinner with your children.

- Practice presence. Resist the urge to put a screen between you and your children on outings, in the car, at a restaurant, when you are food shopping, or while you are waiting in a doctor's office.

- Get moving and exploring. Not just exercising on your own, but engaging in active movement with your children outdoors, playing sports, going on walks, or even just dancing in the kitchen.
- Save yourself first. You set the tone for your family dynamic, which is the foundation for fostering your children's health and happiness. Don't let the behaviors of others in this screen-based world disrupt your ability to parent intentionally.

Pause your reading for now, so you can decide what actions you can take to save yourself first while completing the exercise for Chapter 7 in your Family Playbook.

In the second pillar, we will dive deeper about how to connect and collaborate with your children, strengthening family relationships and fostering skills that can cultivate team leaders and networking skills to thrive in an AI world.

CHAPTER 8

Pillar 2: Connect and Collaborate

Parent Goal: Your children will have good mental health, emotional intelligence, and healthy relationships.

Solution: Increase face-to-face interactions, limit tech disruptions, and connect through real-life shared experiences.

We live in a world where the concept of being an influencer on social media is a coveted title by many children and teens. We are all social beings. Children and adults have a desire to connect with others, gain acceptance, and be part of a community. As adults, the idea that we could stay connected to our high school classmates on Facebook and other adults in our community seemed like an amazing solution. Social media sites made it easier than ever to feel like we were connected to others and gave us the illusion of closeness without our ever picking up the phone. We didn't have to set up coffee dates or go through the expensive process of inviting 500 of our "closest" Facebook friends to lunch just to reconnect. We could do it on our own time, when it fit in our schedule, without any long conversations. We could also tell a bunch of people at once when we got a promotion or when one of our children met a major milestone without spending hours on the phone sharing the information with one person at a time. But something is missing with that, isn't it?

Without deeper conversations and shared experiences, connections with others don't grow. They remain superficial at best. As an adult, you would never expect a Facebook friend or someone you followed on Instagram to visit you in the hospital if you had a major surgery. Maybe a few would come to your wedding if it was open bar, but the cost of travel and giving a wedding gift might be a deterrent.

Research has shown that 29% of teens feel pressure to post things on social media that they believe will result in "likes" and positive comments.[1] This can lead to only sharing what you want others to think about you rather than letting them see who you are. Meanwhile, the people on the receiving end may compare themselves socially to you and your "perfect life" and experience feelings of inadequacy. From another angle, some people engage in "sad phishing," which involves posting something negative about themselves or their feelings in the hope of getting someone to notice they are hurting and provide attention and empathy. But sometimes, that ends up being a red flag for predators and internet trolls to inflict more harm.

If you are a parent with social media accounts, I am guessing you can relate or have seen things like this play out on your social media feed in some form. That is not to say there isn't a space to use social media to make an impact or stay connected with people that you have relationships with in real life. There absolutely is. But often we trade these more superficial experiences for face-to-face relationships more than we would like to believe, including relationships with our children.

Our children are growing up in a world where instead of asking someone for their phone number, they ask for their Instagram or Snapchat. They have just given someone a window into their life who may follow them or send them videos but rarely have a conversation with them. The measuring stick of popularity is based on how many followers you have or if you have had any viral posts. But the way the internet is designed, advertisers and paid influencers cause many of those posts to disappear within hours and your children are back to square one.

Not only are social media and group chats giving the illusion of connection with others at the expense of deeper and closer relationships, they teach us, and our children, to seek significance instead of a true sense of belonging. While significance can signal to a person "I am important and worth attention," belonging is a much deeper feeling of being accepted and valued by others. What may have started as "not feeling important" because of tech disruptions spirals into a focus on constantly trying unsuccessfully to fill that void rather than experiencing interactions that foster a sense of belonging and acceptance and meeting a much deeper human need. What is even more concerning is that more and more children are opting out of opportunities to build social and communication skills in real life, never learning how to effectively navigate interactions with others from diverse backgrounds or cultivate deeper relationships.

Struggling with peer interactions? Join a large group chat, so you don't have to build those skills, but you can still feel part of the group. Don't like asking strangers for help in a store? Just shop online and send your questions or feedback through the customer service email or Google review so you don't feel so emotionally vulnerable. Have difficulty working in a classroom with other peers? Shift to online learning so you can "access the curriculum." While I am saying these things with sarcasm, there is a sad underlying truth in these solutions as more and more children choose isolation over true connection and screen-based interactions over humans. This disrupts the number of opportunities children have in any given day to build social and communication skills. For younger children, language development may be disrupted.[2] Later on, sustained participation in reciprocal conversations may become a struggle when key foundations are missing. Recall that in Chapter 5 we discussed how even in the larger society, people can choose to avoid social interaction with strangers by placing orders online or at kiosks. The rise in social anxiety and difficulty tolerating the behavior of others that think differently is an outgrowth of the option both children and adults have to stay within their comfort zone.

In addition to reducing the number of opportunities to build social and communication skills, key aspects of communication skills are being lost. Albert Mehrabian, a body language researcher, found that 55% of communication is nonverbal, 38% is vocal intonation to express emotion, and 7% is verbal.[3] Talking to someone while looking at your phone disrupts eye contact and use of gestural cues, signaling distraction rather than connection with the person you're talking to.

At what moment did we become so disconnected from each other that many children are not being socialized to read nonverbal cues when these cues are such a powerful influencer of human interaction and connection? Dr. David Novak, a professor and researcher of communication, explains that nonverbal gestures communicate many things like emphasizing a greeting or an emotion of anger as you shake your fist at someone while yelling. He also notes that we use it to coordinate our behavior with another person, possibly to gain favor or create a meaningful connection with them.[4] While talking in-depth about nonverbal communication is not my intention, it is critical to consider how much can be lost in translation when there are tech disruptions during social interactions or the interactions themselves are reduced to soundbites in the form of text messages and memes. Over 90% of communication cues (55% nonverbal and 38% vocal intonation) are lost in text exchanges, especially if you don't know someone's personality well enough. What could *possibly* go wrong?!

I spoke with teachers at a local elementary school during my last workshop who commented that some children were so accustomed to not receiving eye contact from others that when their peers were looking at them from across the room, they perceived it as an aggressive action and told the teacher. Similarly, I observed a young girl with high-functioning autism attempt to navigate social interactions in a pre-K classroom. When the children didn't make eye contact as she attempted to gain their attention, she got close to their faces, invading their personal space to try harder. While this got the teacher's attention and she was redirected for inappropriate behavior, what the teacher failed to notice is that it occurred because the other children either avoided eye contact or weren't aware that it was important to acknowledge her requests to play even though they showed intent by initiating moving toward the play area where the little girl had requested to go. As an occupational therapist, I wonder to myself if children with autism are set up for failure as they learn social rules that their peers haven't been socialized to follow. Luckily, there is still hope. There was a study done including 105 preteens that showed that time away from screen media by attending a screen-free nature camp with increased social interaction may improve comprehension of nonverbal emotional cues. White space, time away from screens, creates the social opportunities necessary for connection and communication.

Without an opportunity to consistently practice face-to-face interactions, children are more vulnerable to:

- Befriending someone in a chatroom that doesn't have their best interests in mind but writes things that make them feel valuable

- Befriending an AI chatbot who mimics social interaction but has no real human emotions to make judgments when a child shares something personal that adults in their life should be made aware of, like having feelings of suicide

- Substituting deeper friendships for large group chats on Discord or group text messages where conversation is reduced to memes, videos, and brief comments in response to media posts

- Struggling with their mental health as they spend more and more time online but less time in social activities where they work with their peers or others in the community towards a common goal

- Struggling to read nonverbal cues or engage in socially appropriate interactions with peers to cultivate friendships. Instead, they recycle the experiences they have had at home where eye contact and reciprocal conversations were inconsistent at best with tech disruptions and follow the social norm of connecting in soundbites.

With the growth of AI, industries have found a way to reduce the number of employees they need while increasing the number of interactions they have with customers. Chatbots feign human emotion, posing as customer service reps, posting on social media, and acting as friends in Snapchat. Our children's development of emotional intelligence, communication skills, and adaptability is a casualty of leaning into tech-based interactions. Yet to thrive in a digital AI world, those uniquely human skills are critical to becoming leaders and creators.

Build Healthy Relationships and the Ability to Function within a Community

We discussed the value of connection for social development. Now let's consider collaboration. Collaboration doesn't mean doing things for someone else. Sometimes it involves space to grow first, and then connecting and collaborating to move forward. Meaning and purpose in life emerge from the struggles we go through as humans in day-to-day, real-life interactions and experiences. What do I mean by this? Think of the struggles that you have endured up to this point in your parenting journey. Your goal is to provide for your children while hopefully, through the combination of parenting decisions that you make, raising your children to become successful adults. Sometimes in the day-to-day business of life, we forget that. We still hope that our struggles and sacrifices will help our children thrive. This hope, followed by seeing our children achieve goals and milestones, gives meaning and value to our experiences. It's what encourages us to persevere as parents. Unexpected life events like divorce, the death of a pet, an unplanned move, a natural disaster, or the loss of a job test our commitment to that goal. As parents, we struggle to rise above those experiences while also helping our children grow through them. Some of us struggle more than others. Some give up or get stuck. But most of us find our way through and continue on with life.

It's important not to wait for a catastrophic event to leave space for the struggles that help your children to build confidence and resilience. Balancing the desire to shield your children from hurt and negative experiences with the opportunity to struggle (yes, I said "opportunity") is a tremendous gift. That is why at times you have to fight your own "mama bear" or "papa bear" protective instincts to create space for this to happen. It starts with small opportunities each day.

Consider the "Work" of Childhood

Toddlers can learn how to put silverware on the table if you encourage them to complete each step. A young child can learn how to transition from plastic hammer and screwdriver playsets to real tools if you give them the materials to make a birdhouse, let them try to apply their knowledge, and then guide them through the pieces they are missing. Recently, I had several middle school boy clients whose parents were concerned about their ability to use a knife safely. Most of them did not have a significant disability that would prevent their learning. However, no one in their lives took a moment to show them the different types of knives that exist in a kitchen and the types of food that each knife is designed for. By learning how to hold an apple versus a piece of chicken while cutting, they were able to expand their knife safety skills. This opened the door to participating in family meal preparation and building skills for independent living.

Why is this important when I am talking about connection and collaboration? In order for children to feel safe in the world, they first need to feel empowered and safe in their bodies. This starts with the ability to independently accomplish goal-oriented activities such as cleaning their rooms, washing dishes, building something, doing yard work, folding laundry, and creating science projects. Do not expect that they will initially do these activities well. We don't expect that for walking or talking, so we should not expect that for anything else. When we teach our children these skills at a young age, knowing it will be a few years before they are actually proficient, we create small struggles that lead to big achievements. We empower them with a sense of accomplishment. These opportunities create a bank of experiences that reminds them that they can act on and interact with their world to achieve something valuable to the greater community.

A 2019 study in the *Journal of Developmental and Behavioral Pediatrics* surveying almost 10,000 children found that children who did chores starting in kindergarten self-reported better self-competence, prosocial behavior, and self-efficacy by third grade than those who did not.[5] Dr. Daniel Amen, child psychologist, physician, and founder of the Amen Clinics, once said in an interview, "There are two words that describe good parenting: firm and kind." By being firm in your expectations and boundaries while being kind in your delivery and support for follow-through, you build your children's confidence and self-esteem. When you do too much for your children, you rob them of their self-esteem. Your presence, guiding your children through this process of doing chores rather than checking off your to-do list while they are occupied in the other room with screens shows your children that they are valuable members of the family. It teaches your children how to work toward the common good of a community while building confidence in their own abilities. You increase your children's capacity for learning what it takes to run a household while building empathy and appreciation for those that do. Your positive feedback and encouragement communicate that they are valued. While there will undoubtedly be grumbles if your children are older and haven't ever done this, be prepared to be consistent in your expectation for participation and meet your children halfway, guiding them through the job until they get more proficient.

Sometimes we, as parents, are trying to get something done like shop, make dinner, or do laundry. We aren't on the phone, but we are busy. During these moments, it's easy to opt for allowing screen time for our children, so we can get the job done faster. However, it is critical that we allow our children to do chores. It might be more time-consuming and less efficient for us, but chores greatly benefit children on multiple levels. For our children, the answer to "less screen time" is often more structured activities. How else do we keep children occupied in something meaningful and off screens, so we can get our ever-increasing workload done? And if we are busy running kids to activities and stealing moments to do work on our laptop, sometimes it's just easier to either hire out the job of housekeeping to someone else or do it ourselves because—let's face it—it's faster and we just "don't have time." To repeat, this is a mistake. Though it might be inefficient and time-consuming for us adults, doing chores greatly benefits children.

When we do more things ourselves because it is easier and faster, we keep our children from learning to live more independently and manage daily tasks. Imagine the time saved and stress relief when you can eventually delegate some of your to-do list, save money on hiring out these tasks, and know without a doubt that you are laying the foundation for your children to become confident and competent adults. Too often the "easy button" is a reaction to the stressors of now rather than focusing on the value of building for the future.

The Value of Play in Childhood

Play is the way that children learn about the world. A baby throws food bowls while sitting in a high chair not to piss you off but to see what happens—the sound it makes, how far it flies, and the impact it has on your emotions. Pretty smart!

In contrast, many neurodiverse children struggle with how to explore the world. They may not initiate. They may need every opportunity explicitly taught. They may need to learn how to explore the world because it is overwhelming and confusing and doesn't make sense to them. But as I said earlier, we all learn about the world through the senses. Sometimes how experiences are wired into the brain is a little faulty and inefficient, but the process is the same for everyone. Create play skills by getting messy with cooking and art projects, roughhousing, and climbing with your children on playground equipment. This not only empowers children to explore the world but creates opportunities for you to give them feedback on their play so that your children learn how to become good playmates. Rough play teaches how much force is okay to use without hurting the other person and social boundaries. Messy play teaches how to get creative without destroying others' property while also learning how different art mediums work. Climbing trees and on playground equipment builds spatial awareness and planning skills while teaching calculated risk-taking, navigating around others, and taking turns. Professor Mariana Brussoni's research about risky play and child development suggests that allowing children to take risks helps them to learn how to avoid excessive risks while simultaneously building their confidence, independence, and resilience.[6]

It is up to you, as a parent, to create the circumstances for those teachable moments. While joining in to play video games with your children may be one way that parents try to bond with their kids or understand what they are playing online, the play that I am referring to is significantly different. This type of play involves opportunities to explore, create ideas with things found in the environment, get sensory feedback from the environment, and help your children figure out how to master the real world. That requires space to learn and create, space to try before being told what to do, space for following your children's lead as long as it is not too dangerous. If there is a way to make an overly-risky idea safer, explain that and show your children how. Then let your children take the risk.

In my occupational therapy sessions with children, I try to be open to any idea that doesn't involve a major safety risk. If children have ideas that I know won't work, I don't tell them. I let them try and then ask them questions to help them figure out why and what to change. If an idea creates a safety issue, I show them how to test the properties of an object and determine why it's not safe. For example, modeling that a foam balance beam is not going to be stable to walk on when resting between a swing and the edge of the ball pit is easily done when I press down on the center of the balance beam and it collapses before their eyes. Then I make a point of saying, "I think this is too soft and squishy to stand on. You might need to pick something stronger to make it work." This teaches children to look around their environment for solutions to problems and adapt their plan as they gather information about how their bodies and the objects around them interact. This especially comes in handy with smart and strong-willed children who won't accept no for an answer when they believe something is possible. In this way, I don't limit their opportunities but rather foster exploration that empowers them to make better judgments and builds their confidence.

Parents watch in amazement as their children transform from anxious and afraid or resistant and controlling to collaborative and adaptable. This empowers parents to carry over these strategies at home to foster more growth. Sometimes the children with the strongest wills end up being the best leaders and change-makers. They don't take no for an answer but are equipped with the knowledge of how to make something possible. This can't happen if children experience the world through YouTube videos and video games. The physical world creates opportunities for multisensory experiences that help children thrive if we don't disrupt the opportunities but facilitate instead. We need to raise leaders and creators rather than consumers and followers if we want to give our children the ability to thrive in a digital world.

As a parent, you are both the guide and the boundary-setter in play. At times, play requires that you remind controlling children that having ideas for their own body is fine, but you get to make choices about your body and what you want to do. Helping anxious children find a way to try to initiate play requires encouraging these children to tap into their "bravery brain" and telling their "worry brain" to be quiet. While these children may only take one step on the balance beam at the playground on the first attempt, it is still an attempt and an act of "bravery" from their perspective. Praise it while not expecting them to walk all the way across. Remember, progress not perfection. Setting boundaries with a child that often plays too rough while showing the child what they can do instead to keep the game going allows them to learn how to become a better playmate. Does this mean it's better for children to play with adults? No. But it does mean that playing with your children allows them to experience adaptive play and learn skills that they can bring to the playground, playdates, and birthday parties to use with their peers. Expecting them to always entertain themselves or play with their siblings as you check off your endless to-do list but rarely creating space to play as a family sets them up to learn from peers that also may lack these skills and experience more negative feedback from others.

We often tell children, "It's not whether you win or lose, it's how you play the game." That means nothing when the digital world teaches exactly the opposite in video games. We know that, in life, it's the people who make themselves irreplaceable who are less likely to get outsourced. Strive to foster skills that empower your children and allow them to become good playmates for life. Winning and achievement is a goal to strive for because it meets the human need for growth and contribution to the community. But the greater goal as a parent is for your children to learn skills that make them secure in their identities and abilities while being able to engage with others in ways that are socially desirable. These uniquely human traits cannot be outsourced to AI and remain highly sought after by employers.

If we want our children to have more job opportunities, the ability to connect and collaborate with people while fostering creativity and innovation is critical to competing for jobs in a digital and AI world.

Choosing Human Connection over Chatbots and Videos

Success in a digital world means that we need to cultivate uniquely human skills. Meanwhile, industries are using AI to scale their businesses and reduce the number of employees needed to do the job. We see this currently in the use of chatbots for customer service, generating images, and using ChatGPT to construct essays and media posts—just to name a few. Coaching professionals scaling their businesses are beginning to embrace the concept of using AI mentors, so they can effectively clone themselves and their knowledge to offer to others without hiring additional coaches. It would be fair to say that industries are encouraging us to interact with AI as much as possible and reducing the number of human interactions that we actually experience on a day-to-day basis. As I mentioned in the previous chapter, this has major implications for the development of our children and essentially trains them to get used to interacting with AI technology that is devoid of emotion and does not have the ability to recognize human nuances in tone and nonverbal communication that may be very important.

Many of us have already experienced videos labeled as deepfakes. This technology is a type of artificial intelligence (AI) that creates realistic but fake media content using algorithms and facial-mapping software to manipulate or synthesize faces and speech. It's also easy to photoshop images and make things appear different than what they are. Posts and short video clips don't last long enough to send up red flags to the viewer unless they are able to see the nuances in the video edits. But at the same time, there is AI technology that I could use as an entrepreneur to create a video that is overlaid with the AI version of my voice, so all I have to do is upload a text document to create a voiceover for a video or podcast episode. Could be a time-saver for sure! It would be naive to think that our children will never encounter videos, posts, and podcasts made like this or even that they won't learn to create them. The question I would like you to consider is: Do children, or even many adults for that matter, have sufficient knowledge of themselves, the world, and face-to-face human interactions during work and play to tell the difference?

One of our roles as parents is to guide our children towards healthy relationships, interactions, and thought patterns. In a digital world, children are being influenced, not just by predators, but by the algorithms taking the faces of chatbots, AI-produced video content, and social media feeds. These algorithms don't read human emotion; they analyze data. This means if your child watches a video with a sad song in the background, your child may see ten more videos with "sad songs," but some of them may promote self-harm and suicide. Not exactly the choice you would make if you were listening to the radio with your child and you realized it was time to change the song to something more positive and upbeat. Businesses race to harness the power of artificial intelligence to save money, increase profits, streamline tasks, and reduce overhead. Child development is simply not a priority. The side effect of this is that while adults may be "harnessing the power of AI" to succeed, our children are developing in a world that effectively reduces the number of human interactions they have in a given day.

We have no idea how many interactions a human needs to develop social awareness, communication skills, and emotional intelligence. We never had to think about it too much because when we were growing up, the opportunities were always there en masse in the daily experiences of life. We do know that it varies with every person, depending on their neurodiversity, cognitive ability, and environmental factors that give them the opportunity to interact with people who have emotional intelligence, communication, and social skills that are above their own. This is why 3-, 4-, and 5-year-olds are together in a preschool classroom—so that they can learn from each other. This is also the benefit of large families; older children have more skills than the younger children. Gallup polls from 1936 to 1967 showed that families favored having three or more children through the post-World War Two baby boom. While the average peaked at 3.6 during that period, it plummeted to 1.8 by 1980 with shifts in societal norms and the number of women in the workplace.[7] Given that the size of US families averages one to two children combined with the fact that the number of engagements with technology over people is increasing, we can't possibly know the rate at which the lack of opportunities for human connection and collaboration are impacting our children. Mental health data clearly tells us that our children are already struggling with lack of emotional intelligence, social interaction skills, resilience, and adaptability. Reducing engagement with technology in the world as a whole and creating opportunities for human interaction and real-life experiences increases a child's connection to humans while building the foundation for confidence and a sense of purpose.

In the next chapter, I will teach you more about the value of movement from a sensory perspective. Not all movement is created equal, but if you know its value, you can harness its power to foster self-regulation, focus, attention, and skill development in your children.

> Before moving on, get out your Family Playbook, and consider the suggestions that might be realistic for you to try with your own children as you complete the Chapter 8 exercise.

CHAPTER 9

Pillar 3: Move with a Purpose

*Parent Goal: Your children will build
emotional and mental well-being.*

*Solution: Create a strong physiological foundation
by balancing screen time, sleep, and movement.*

Technology has put us on a superhighway for getting more done in less time, but is this really helping our children? With all that you have read so far, I am sure you would agree that the answer is no. Children's brains and bodies are still developing. As you learned in the previous chapter, novel experiences and exploration followed by consistent opportunities to practice skills and adapt to change are critical to that process. Raising leaders and creators rather than allowing our children to become consumers and followers in a digital and AI world is an intentional process.

This is the chapter where I am going to put on my sensory integrative occupational therapist hat and give you a brief lesson on development from a sensory perspective. I promise, I will try to keep it brief. I am sharing it so that everything I say in the rest of the chapter will make a whole lot more sense.

Too often we focus on the skills and milestones kids are achieving because that is how society has been able to measure if a child is on track with things like language development, motor skills, and academic knowledge. The fact is that the devil is in the details. You can have a child that is taught a lot of language but struggles to communicate experiences. You can have a child that has certain motor skills like climbing or doing jumping jacks but struggles to participate in gym class or play sports. You can have kids with amazing memories but terrible reasoning skills. How does this happen?

The brain learns by connecting and reconnecting information infinitely in many different ways to adapt to and make sense of the world. It doesn't run on linear algorithms like a computer does. This is a big part of being uniquely human. The way the brain collects information is through the senses. You know, the ones we all learned about in elementary school but were never told why they helped us learn. In addition to the five senses of touch, taste, sight, hearing, and smell, we have two additional senses: proprioception (muscles and joints) and the vestibular (balance and gravity) system. These hidden senses give us information about how our body is moving, how much force we need to do something like open a bag of chips, which way is up, how fast we are moving, and in what direction we are moving through space.

Beyond that, the vestibular system sends messages to the limbic system for alertness and attention while also promoting memory formation.[1] It is kind of like a keystone in an archway. It works together with all the other senses to give the brain enough information to determine how the body should respond in a given situation.

Information from the senses travels through the brain stem into the cerebellum and other parts of the brain necessary for analyzing and interpreting information. We used to think that the cerebellum was the part of the brain responsible for helping us process motor information and support coordination. This is what I learned in my neurology class in college in 1999. We now know that the cerebellum is basically a *little brain,* constantly processing sensory and motor information and connecting with other parts of the brain to facilitate development of language, reasoning, body control, visual spatial skills, reading, writing, and executive functions.[2]

Take this example: If you have ever been in the woods in the dark—maybe feeling a bit scared—your senses heighten. Suddenly, you hear every sound, and anything that touches your skin makes you jump. Your eyes start darting around in space, scanning the environment for signs of a threat. Your vestibular system gives you your sense of space, so your eyes know where to look. As you turn your head, your heart rate rises. Blood begins pumping to your muscles and they tense, getting ready to figure out which way for you to run, if necessary. If you decide running out of the woods is your best option, you find yourself telling every detail of your near-death experience to the first person who will listen.

The senses are always working together to both take in information for the brain to organize and to execute adaptive motor responses based on that information. This is how all humans are wired.

Why Should You Care About All of This?

Let's go back to the speed of technology. The easier it is to get information visually and auditorily from a screen, the less we move and explore the world around us through our senses. But if all of development is dependent on this brain process, then it follows that children who live in a digital world are having a fundamentally different experience than the generations before them.

I mentioned earlier that the rise in screen-based activities during COVID catapulted us toward embedding more and more technology into daily experiences such as Zoom and Google Meet, online gaming playdates, Google Classroom for elementary schoolers, online ordering, and using videos for classroom movement breaks. There are now two generations of children (Gen Z and Gen Alpha) struggling more than the generations before with self-regulation, learning in the classroom, social skills, and play skills. They are less resilient and easily overwhelmed. One thing is for sure: My colleagues and I are not lacking for business. At the risk of putting myself out of a job, I would rather let you in on my secrets if it means that more children grow up happy, healthy, and able to succeed.

While I can't say that only moving less has created the challenges kids are facing, it is a key consideration when it comes to building the foundation for success: If you work with the natural way that the brain and body learn, you will not only build your children's skills, you will be preparing your children for life in a digital world.

So Should You Just Have Your Kids Run Around More?

Not exactly. In a digital world, time is precious and limited, so it's important to be intentional about sensory and movement opportunities. In the past, we didn't really have to think about it as much because not having the internet naturally led to more trips to the library, more backyard playdates, and more downtime to get creative.

In the wellness space, the focus on health and fitness for adults has increased along with the number of coaches claiming that their program is the best one to lose weight and get in shape. Fitness trackers and gym memberships abound, with people chasing step counts and constantly committing (and recommitting) to getting to the gym regularly. I don't use a fitness tracker. For me, it's just a reminder of all the ways I am failing at exercise.

Recommended amounts of exercise for the general population are 60 minutes daily for children and 30 minutes daily for adults.[3] There has been consideration of increasing those numbers since so many people spend, at minimum, four to six hours behind a computer for work, school, and leisure. I would argue that so many of us are overscheduled, stretched too thin, and multitasking constantly that we struggle to organize our day to dedicate 30 to 60 minutes to focused exercise.

Parents sign their children up for after-school activities that often take up multiple afternoons a week. Yet, as I mentioned earlier, obesity, mental health issues, social difficulties, and symptoms of attention deficits are all rising in children. When we look at the data, it's not hard to see why. Twenty-six percent of tweens ages 8-12 are spending four to eight hours per day and 29% of teens spend more than eight hours viewing entertainment media.[4] Couple this with doing school work online, the number is much higher. If kids are awake, on average, from 7 a.m. to 9 p.m., that means over 50% of the day could be spent on screens while only 7% of the day is spent moving if we assume kids are exercising the recommended 60 minutes. So I want to challenge you to rethink how you think about movement in your day.

Let's start with the basics. Research shows that generally speaking, there are three kinds of movement we should all have in our day:

1. **Movement that incorporates rhythm, pressure, and respiration.** Activities with these elements include tai chi, yoga, and modern dance and are good examples of this type of movement. Research shows that these elements specifically reduce cortisol levels in the body responsible for stress and "cell death" (that refers to the killing of brain cells when in a constant state of stress).[5,6,7] This can cause the limbic system, the part of the brain responsible for emotional and physiological regulation, to shrink and dopamine regulation to get disrupted, impacting motivation, concentration, and happiness.[8]

2. **Movement that increases your heart rate.** Think activation of the vestibular (movement) and proprioceptive (muscle and joint) systems. Cardiovascular exercise increases the production of brain-derived neurotrophic hormone factor (BDNF).[9] This is the hormone responsible for stimulating connections in the brain. More connections mean more opportunities to develop and refine the complex connections in our brains that help us adapt to the world around us.

Aerobic exercise also releases dopamine at an appropriate level to enhance focus, attention, and self-regulation.

3. **Goal-directed movement.** This can include things like sports but can also be any activity that has a goal or intention behind it like a soccer drill, shuttle run, boxing, doing chores, or helping with yard work. Games and activities that require a person to work toward a certain goal help build the executive functions of adaptability and goal-directed behavior.[10] More than sit-ups or pushups, they help you learn how to focus, filter out distractions, and adjust to the demands of activities—all very valuable skills when it comes to succeeding at life.

This research led to the creation of my Body Activated Learning™ Framework for classroom teachers, parents, and other professionals. Many of us think of exercise as a way to keep our muscles and heart healthy, lose weight, or reduce stress. However, exercise actually does so much more than that if it's the right kind. Movement activates the senses, which, in turn, regulate our energy and arousal, meaning how awake and alert or calm and relaxed we are at any given moment. It can be used to reduce stress and cortisol levels, or provide energy to the brain for alertness and attention. When movement activates multiple senses and is goal-directed, it trains the body to adapt to activity demands such as playing sports, getting dressed in the morning, doing chores, or sitting at a desk and writing.

In 1949, Donald Hebb, a Canadian neuropsychologist known for his work in the field of associative learning, coined the phrase, "Neurons that fire together wire together." It has come to be known in the field of neuroplasticity as Hebb's Axiom. What this means is that negative experiences and failure can get hard-wired in the brain just as easily as positive experiences. Children with low coordination don't magically figure out how to get better at sports or put their clothes on without sitting on the floor to avoid losing their balance. But when we set up opportunities to practice movement that is goal-directed and also improves balance and coordination, children are able to effectively participate in activities with their peers, expand their independent life skills, and figure out how to adapt when something about the activity changes. An easy way to think about this is that practicing a soccer drill to build ball control develops one foundation while getting on the field and learning how to control the ball while navigating around the other players on the way to the goal forces adaptability. With all this in mind, let's think of movement as falling into four categories: energizing, restoring, activating, and regrouping.

Energize

Movement that falls into this category is unpredictable, can involve moving faster and slower, and engages the muscles. It doesn't have a lot of hand-eye coordination because it is meant to be sensory input that wakes up the body and gets it ready for the next activity. The ear converts sounds (through the auditory system) and movement (through the vestibular system) into energy for the brain. According to Dr. Alfred Tomatis, an ear, nose, and throat doctor well known for his development of the Tomatis Method, the ear provides 50% of the energy to the brain.[11] Think about how music often makes you want to move and dance. Think about how awake you feel after a thrill ride, dancing, or playing a sport. Unpredictability in movement, such as going fast and slow or changing directions as you move, increases alertness as the brain reacts to those changes in movement patterns, signaling the body to "wake up and respond." This increases blood flow to the muscles, speeds up heart rate, and increases vigilance (meaning you look around and pay closer attention to what is going on around you) so that the body can respond quickly to whatever is coming. Giving resistance to the muscles gives them the extra sensory feedback they need to respond. Did you ever feel taller or stand up straighter when you finished a workout? That is your postural muscles responding to the extra sensory input.

Here are some examples of energizing movements:

- Jumping on a trampoline and doing tricks
- Riding a scooter or a bike around the neighborhood or obstacles
- Dancing freestyle to an upbeat song
- Spinning on a merry-go-round
- Rolling, flipping, and somersaulting
- Using resistance bands or free weights while walking or doing an aerobic workout

While it's tempting to encourage a child to sit down and not draw attention to themselves or act impulsively in public, impulsive movement and moving around may be signs that a child is seeking this movement and needs more of it in a structured way to channel it for focus and attention. In contrast, children who are overly sedentary may not seek out energizing movement because they don't have the motor skills to move efficiently or their energy level/level of alertness is too low. In the case of children diagnosed with attention deficit hyperactivity disorder, you have hyperactive, inattentive, and combined types. All of these children benefit from "energy" to their brains through movement, whether they seek it (hyperactive) or are "zoning out" (inattentive). They struggle to regulate their dopamine levels,[12] something energizing aerobic exercise supports. The same goes for children who spend much of their day sitting in a classroom and on couches playing video games.

Restore

Movement in this category incorporates rhythm, pressure, and respiration for calming and stress reduction. Rhythm, like rocking a baby to sleep, decreases stress hormones. Pressure, like a big hug, does the same thing while also releasing serotonin (the happy hormone).[13] Respiration, like deep breathing, slows the heart rate while also providing calming pressure to the body via the lungs.[14] Engaging in activities that provide opportunities for rhythm, pressure, and respiration (deep breathing) move the body into a calm and relaxed state. This is critical for managing stress, recovering from being upset, and creating emotional space to allow for reasoning and rational responses over tantrums and aggression. When chronic stress and dysregulation disrupt the function of the dopamine system, restorative movement can help bring it back into balance.

The challenge with deep breathing is that not every child knows how to do it, so sometimes focusing more on rhythm and pressure is a better idea initially. If a child can blow out, forced exhales naturally facilitate deep breaths in. This means blowing a feather can be more effective for regulation than telling a child to "calm down and take deep breaths." Focusing on the feather has the added benefit of shifting their point of focus away from an upsetting experience. For neurodiverse children and typical children alike, building the skill of blowing can be invaluable in supporting self-regulation.

Rhythm comes in many forms:

- Walking
- Tapping
- Repeating a movement such as moving a medicine ball from one side of the room and back again multiple times
- Rocking in a chair
- Swaying side to side to slow music

Rhythm can be done faster initially and then gradually slowed down to 60 beats per minute to match the speed of a resting heart rate. This is important when you have children who "have a lot of energy" but still need to be able to slow down to focus or fall asleep at night.

Pressure provides calming input through the skin using things like:

- Weighted blankets
- Hugs
- Getting "squished" with a pillow or beanbag
- Progressive muscle relaxation (tensing up different body parts as much as you can and then releasing)

Respiration, specifically encouraging deep breathing, may include:

- Blowing foam blow darts at a target (think the breathing version of Nerf guns)
- Blowing a cotton ball across the table with a straw
- Taking deep breaths
- Blowing up a balloon
- Blowing bubbles

Activate

Jim Kwik says, "When your body moves, your brain grooves." This is an easier phrase to remember than Hebb's Axiom (and easier to explain to your children!). That phrase has stuck with me and I have passed on that sentiment in almost every lecture or workshop I present. Activating exercise is goal-directed and should engage a variety of senses. Hand-eye coordination is a necessary part of teaching the eyes to guide what the body is doing. Activities that engage the hands and fingers build the foundation for self-help skills and pencil use. Activities that require active listening and motor responses build skills for direction-following and auditory attention. The inherent rewards associated with achieving goals naturally boosts dopamine levels in a healthy way.

The list of activities that fall in this category are endless and vary by age and ability. Some examples include:

- Ball play (catching, throwing into a basketball hoop, kicking into a goal)
- Setting up an obstacle course with items around the house
- Doing chores like mopping and window-washing
- Learning a dance with hand and body movements
- Playing tabletop games that require pinching, pulling, pushing or building things that require use of tools, tape dispensers, or staplers

As you can see, these movements are designed to accomplish a goal. They facilitate the activation of the senses to engage in purposeful movement for skill development. One of my friends often comments that he is so active in his daily life, he doesn't really need to go to the gym. On any given day, he may be working on a car, helping a friend clear trees in their yard, doing roof repairs, or building something.

If we consider the lives of the Old Order Amish and ultraconservative Amish groups, we can say something similar about them. They are always working together, doing some sort of project in their community involving building and farming. They engage in a lot of goal-directed activity. These groups often avoid modern technology. While in many ways these conservative groups appear to be at the opposite extreme of the rest of American society, we can take a few pointers. They have skills that allow them to build thriving farms and businesses working with their hands without being technology-dependent.

I currently have a child client who struggles with planning and sequencing but loves intense physical activity such as hockey. He enjoys helping on building projects but hyper-focuses on the power tools because he struggles with how to plan, visualize, and organize the steps needed to accomplish the task. When the project is about 80% complete, a light bulb goes off in his mind, and suddenly he can see what to do. Immediately, his investment in the activity increases because there is a manageable level of planning. While he is not yet ready to conceptualize, plan, and build anything on his own, his love of physical activity makes these kinds of multisensory learning opportunities a perfect match to fill in the gaps in spatial perception, visualization, and planning. In school, the planning and organizational demands expected from a middle schooler are above his current abilities, making it hard for him to participate.

If you have a neurodiverse child, this example may resonate with you. But even if you have a younger child who would not be expected to have fully-baked plans, setting up frequent opportunities for hands-on learning in the kitchen, in the yard, at the grocery store, etc., is critical. In a digital world more and more children struggle with writing and fine motor skill development as well as following through with multi-step motor tasks independently. Intentionally engaging them in interactive games, baking, chores, building projects, etc., provides critical opportunities for development of posture, coordination, and spatial awareness while building the executive function skills of adaptability and goal-directed behavior.

Regroup

Regrouping incorporates stretching, breathing, and vision breaks. Stretching is critical not just to reduce sports injuries but to head off back and neck pain associated with too much screen time. Tensing and fixing (like hiking up your shoulders when holding a video game controller) while sitting for long periods in front of a screen can lead to discomfort and irritability. When visual fatigue sets in, it's natural to tense neck and back muscles as your eyes strain to focus. Posture and vision are inseparable; when one is affected, the other is too. That is why both stretching and vision breaks are so critical.

Vision breaks may look like:

- Cupping both eyes with your hands and staring into the black for 30 seconds
- Taking a walk outside, where distance vision is required instead of focusing on a screen
- Turning off the lights and taking a break in a dark space
- Going inside a tunnel or under a blanket to hide

Whether brief or a whole activity, vision breaks are critical for maintaining eye health[15] as well as improving visual endurance for the duration of the school day. When children's eyes begin to fatigue, they may experience light sensitivity, start seeing double, or no longer be able to focus on school work. Combining vision breaks with stretching reduces tension throughout the whole body. Intentional breathing further helps with relaxation and recovery from skill demands.

You can put these elements together in simple movement sequences to try out at home. Visit the Body Activated Learning™ Playlist on the Sensational Achievements Youtube channel to see some examples and watch a few videos on Body Activated Learning™. Or you can start by noticing where there are opportunities throughout the day for energizing, restoring, activating, and regrouping.

Younger children don't typically engage in traditional exercise, but they do run, swim, climb, jump, play outdoor games, play sports, and enjoy building and creating. If your children are neurodiverse, work with a therapy team to see how you can incorporate these types of movements into your children's programs at a manageable level, especially when they can't access typical sports and dance classes.

Research completed on using Body Activated Learning™ exercises in fourth grade classrooms shows some improvements in reading and math scores after only six weeks.[16] The children who received specialized learning supports made the greatest improvement in the shortest period of time. To me, this reinforces that movement is a necessary part of supporting self-regulation, attention, and learning. When we move intentionally throughout the day in short bursts, we can optimize brain and body functions for academic and personal success. The feedback from both the teachers and the children was positive. The children voted strongly to continue to do the exercises beyond the six-week research project. They reported that their attention and focus improved even more than the teachers perceived it did. The teachers had a different take-away. The results from incorporating vision breaks were so noticeable to them that they started using vision breaks spontaneously throughout the school day outside of the research protocol. Next thing I knew, the district placed a handbook order for multiple schools so they could use the program with more students. This shows that when you give children the right movement—movement that they didn't even know they needed until it was offered—their ability to engage in the work of childhood expands.

Digital Detoxing

The last critical element of purposeful movement is planned digital detoxes. Digital detoxes are intentional periods throughout the day or week where the family puts away their phones, tablets, and computers to do something together. This could be playing a board game, taking a walk around the block after dinner, or going to the park with the family dog. Tech-free activities, while they may be unpopular at first, provide a critical opportunity for the brain to recover from excessive stimulation and dopamine disruptors. Too much dopamine can make non-screen activities feel boring and slow. However, regular digital detoxes can modulate dopamine levels,[17] making it easier to sustain participation in non-screen activities that build focus, sustained attention, and problem-solving skills.

With low-stimulation digital detoxes, children and teens alike may grumble and complain initially, but I have heard more than one success story when families stick to a digital detox plan for even one evening per week. A teacher reported to me that her teenage sons complained and teased her when she decided to have a screen-free weekly family game night. After just two weeks, they expanded their activities to include exercising together and reading books, screen-free, of course. The complaints stopped, and they began enjoying each other's company again. They were able to experience the positive social and multisensory experiences that regulate dopamine levels in a healthy way to foster focus, creativity, and engagement.

You may be tempted to sign your children up for lots of after-school activities to reduce screen-time opportunities. Even if your child isn't signed up for sports or dance classes, bike riding, playgrounds, hiking, and backyard obstacle courses are all free, and all of them can be tech-free if you set an intention and practice presence. This includes parents putting away their phones and practicing presence too. Free play and self-directed learning fosters exploration and creativity—critical skills for future leaders and creators living a digital and AI world. This is why so many Silicon Valley parents see value in Montessori and Waldorf School learning approaches. Often, free play is even better than all the activities you could sign your child up for because doing less while remaining active can decrease a child's total load of commitments, school, screen time, and homework that at times can feel overwhelming. The more chronic stress a person experiences, the more "cell death" occurs in the brain. Shrinkage in the limbic system (the part of the brain that supports emotional regulation), decreases a person's ability to handle stress better in the future.[18]

Another problem with overscheduling is that it can lead to downtime in front of a screen at night to decompress, which can also affect sleep patterns. Melatonin production is suppressed by the blue light emanating from screens.[19] Doing activities late into the evening multiple days of the week increases conflicts with getting the sleep the brain needs to consolidate and organize the information of the day for thinking and learning. Habits and routines that support the physiological foundation for regulation and emotional well-being are critical to optimizing your children's performance and success across all areas of life.

Be Legendary: Raising Kids to Thrive in a Digital and AI World

A legendary coach both inspires and expects greatness from the team. The coach's responsibility is to put together practice drills, team-building activities, and cultural expectations for the group that help to raise them to the highest versions of themselves. As parents, this is also part of what we do. While most of us aren't raising professional athletes, we are raising the industry leaders of tomorrow and the creators that will spur the next transformational age. As parents, we are in charge of the culture of our home. We decide the activities we sign kids up for or the amount of time they spend with family and friends. We create the schedule and the flow of the day for our children. We create opportunities for multisensory learning and purposeful movement. Sometimes doing less is more if it's intentional. By incorporating the principles of Body Activated Learning™ and building in digital detoxes, you will foster yet another success habit that will serve your children for a lifetime.

Pillar 4 is all about harnessing multisensory opportunities in the world while intentionally choosing to not hit the widely available "easy button" with technology, so we can raise leaders and creators with uniquely human skills, not consumers and followers.

> But before you do that, turn to Chapter 9 of your Family Playbook, and make an action plan to get moving and digitally detox. Plus, I will reveal the little-known secret of why achieving dopamine regulation is key for raising leaders and creators, not just consumers in a digital and AI world.

CHAPTER 10

Pillar 4: Learn and Grow Sensationally

Parent Goal: Your children will experience academic success and success in learning.

Solution: Opt for multisensory learning tools over digital solutions when available.

In the previous chapter, I explained how the brain doesn't work in straight lines. It thrives by connecting and reconnecting information in infinite ways. A fundamental truth for all humans, regardless of neurodiversity, cultural, or economic background, is that we are all sensory beings. This is how we explore the world, experience it, and learn from it. While children do rely on adults to help them make sense of everything (as evidenced by children going through a phase of asking, "Why?" so often that it might drive you to insanity), the process of learning is not about exposure to content. It's about teaching kids how to think, experiment, and problem-solve. That means making sure multisensory experiences are present in as many opportunities for learning as possible, both in and out of the classroom.

The 1983 report "A Nation at Risk: The Imperative for Educational Reform from the United States National Commission on Excellence in Education" suggested that the then current state of education in America was not preparing children to meet the demands of the workforce and that our children were not as advanced as those in other countries.[1] It set the standards for the length of a school day, what subjects and how much of a subject should be taught in high school, and expectations for teacher qualifications, and it encouraged raising standards for college admission but focused mainly on high school.

In 1989, the United States began focusing on developing content standards for each grade level and standardized testing to measure competency. This happened gradually over a period of ten to 11 years. By 2002, No Child Left Behind furthered this vision, expanding requirements for competency for all children and often tying funding for schools to students performing well on standardized tests.[2] In 2010, we saw the advent of the Common Core State Standards Initiative to bring consistency to education across states for grades K to 12.[3] This was made possible by the fact that the internet made a common core of knowledge and content available in all states. Now we see that a few colleges are abandoning SAT and ACT testing as a primary way to determine college admission with test-optional college applications, but standardized testing is still part of public education and tied to school funding. Teachers feel pressured to teach to the standardized tests even if their students are economically, neurologically, and culturally diverse.

While each of these initiatives has received mixed reviews from teachers, parents, and administrators, we can agree that the initial question raised was "How do we get our children to be ready to compete in the workforce?" Over time, it became clear that the workforce was no longer local but global. Many jobs can now be done virtually from home or are projected to be outsourced to artificial intelligence if they haven't been already. Skilled laborers and tradesmen are becoming the new millionaires despite once being looked down upon for not going to college.[4]

There continues to be significant diversity in the way that schools educate children. This is a topic for another book. But what is important to note is that advances in medical technology, shifts in societal norms, and increasing cultural diversity mean that we are educating classrooms full of students who have English as a second language and families that don't speak English, children that may have been born premature with underdeveloped nervous systems, and children born to older parents who have a higher risk of having children with certain types of disabilities. We are struggling to support each child's ability to learn in the school environment while balancing that with government standards and expectations.

This struggle is not going away. Schools have tried online learning programs to adapt to each student's level so they progress at their own pace. Schools have adopted preset curriculums to ensure that content outlined in the standards is being introduced, and schools are adapting methods to those outlined in the curriculum. In my experience observing in classrooms and talking with educators, they have reduced homework expectations as families have said it's too much or too difficult when a parent doesn't speak English or have complained that it is impossible with after-school activity demands. They have instituted modified work and modified grading for students with disabilities, boosting performance metrics on paper, but only on paper. They have created robust English language learners programs.

The number of children needing individualized educational programs has risen nationally from 12% to 15%.[5] Parents who have the ability to seek out private schools that are a better fit for their children's needs try to do that. Some parents find that even in private schools that appear to have best-fit programming, their children still struggle. There is no easy answer. This educational mindset has been evolving for 40 years, so it's no easy task to shift course. It will take a combination of parental pressure and governmental shifts in public policy to update the public education system for a neurodiverse generation of learners who need skills to thrive in a digital world.

What is clear is that there have been very few initiatives adopted by public school systems that reflect what neuroscientists have known for years—preparing for adulthood is not just about learning facts and figures. The brain is comprised of a network of regions that work in concert to accomplish a given task. Its plasticity and malleability for learning and function should not be underestimated if children are given the right tools to succeed.

Going back to our fears and our goals for our children, let me take a moment to remind you of our "whys" as they relate to learning:

- We want our kids to experience academic success.
- We want our kids to live independently and manage daily tasks.
- We want our kids to achieve financial independence.

- We want our children to have job opportunities.
- We want our kids to be successful learners.

In the sections that follow, I will show how you can shift your lens in the way you view learning to read, learning math and finance, how you teach your teen to drive, and how you promote executive functions and up-level your parenting strategies. You have my permission to skip sections that don't apply to you yet and come back later to read them as your children grow.

Learn and Grow Habit 1:
Up-Level Your Child's Academic Learning Experience

Parent Goal: Your children will experience academic success.

Solution: More opportunities for multisensory learning rather than more "leveled learning" math and reading games, videos, and assistive technology to compensate for missing skills.

How often—when you look up information on how to do something—do you end up clicking on a video where someone explains it and shows you step by step how to do something? Convenient, isn't it? I have learned how to change oil in my car, replace air filters, prune roses, make better donuts, decorate a cake—lots of useful things. It doesn't really occur to me that I should go to the library and take out a book on subject matters such as "basic car maintenance," "basic gardening tips by season," or "the best tips and tricks for cake decoration." In fact, I am pretty sure there are blog titles out there somewhere on each of these topics.

For children, watching videos to learn and figure out how to do something isn't in and of itself a bad thing. Many children do much better when they see something versus only hearing instructions. Many children are very reliant on images in books to understand the context of what they are reading or the process of how to do something as their language skills and bank of experiences evolve. The Lego enthusiasts of the world love buying kits and following the 40-page full-color step-by-step instructions to build something that is listed for ages 12-plus when they are only 6. But there is something bigger to consider rather than just the day-to-day convenience of a good two- to five-minute video that teaches you how to be a "hacker" by figuring out how to do on your own what a company gets paid to provide as a service.

Some of the child clients I work with struggle with drawing. There is a great YouTube channel called Art for Kids. One of the kids I work with loves how the dad/artist in the videos show you step by step how to make haunted houses, sea creatures, crazy Christmas trees, and all sorts of other things. Initially, the videos may as well have been on fast forward. He had no idea how to draw the elements the right size or put them in the right place, but he hated the idea of trying to draw his own picture even more, so I compromised. We struck a balance between watching the video in three-second increments and him copying my drawings step by step on a large whiteboard, using whole body movements and a large space to help him understand how each piece of a drawing fit together. Eventually, he graduated to being able to look at a picture and figure out his own step-by-step approach to drawing using a piece of paper. The biggest challenge for him was understanding what part of the drawing to do first, second, third, etc., and then figuring out where each part met another. But if I stuck with just letting him pick a video and follow along, he never would have built the confidence or the skills to attempt to draw a picture about the amazing hotel he stayed in on vacation for show and tell.

Most people's brains excel at processing the world through images and pictures. In fact, 80% of the information we get from the world comes in through our visual system.[6] That leaves about 20% coming from our other senses. Not very much, but that 20% changes everything. It provides essential information about the shape, weight, and texture of objects. It sends messages to the body to adapt based on this information to be able to manipulate materials, judge how far to cut down the rose stem, determine how much to squeeze the piping bag to get just the right amount of icing for a cake design, or figure out if a bolt is tight enough. In short, without the information from all the other senses, we can't translate what we see on a video to real life and develop any degree of proficiency with it.

The other skills that get built when we don't have a video to show us step by step how to do something are problem-solving, adaptability, visualization, and sustained effort or attention to a task at hand. You have seen these words repeated earlier in this book. These are uniquely human skills that can't be outsourced to technology. Step-by-step tutorials may be helpful, but we want children to be able to take things apart, engage with the materials, and figure out how things work. By doing this, they gain an understanding of how things work together to achieve a larger goal. If they focus on just one part or one step, they will never develop the executive function skills to visualize processes and workflows in an AI-powered world.

For example, if you are used to just setting plates down in front of your children at dinner, how will they learn to watch the clock for when it's getting close to dinner, prep food for cooking, pour the milk without spilling, use a serving spoon to plate their meal, or set the table to prepare to sit down and eat? Participating in coming up with ideas, developing a plan, and putting it into action comes from engaging in the entire sequence of events, not just showing up to eat.

Similarly, when children are given checklists to stay on task at school, they are just referencing one task at a time on the list. No one is working with them to expand their ability to know what they have to do for a given project, get the materials they need, and sit down to complete the work. I have yet to see a goal on an individualized education plan for teaching children to become the list-creators rather than the list-followers. Yet when the expectation of independence suddenly emerges in middle school, increases in high school, and then culminates in adulting in the real world, many still seem to hold out hope that children will grow up and these abilities will emerge naturally. That used to be the case in a lower tech world, but I would argue that it's not anymore.

Trade Videos and E-Books for Paperbacks and Hardcovers

So why should children read a book instead of watching a video? Book-reading is a multisensory experience. "What do I mean by that?" you ask. There is so much that comes from reading a book compared to watching a video. Think about a book and what it takes to get, read, and use a book to learn something:

First, we have to go to the library or the bookstore.

We always used to have to walk, drive, or ride a bike to a physical store or library (movement through space) before e-books and audiobooks.

If we used the alphabetized cards and the Dewey Decimal System, we were only able to write down so many titles on a piece of scrap paper for our library search (limited volume of information to gather and retain). We walked through the maze of the library or bookstore, mapping out the location of where certain subjects and fiction books were located (more movement as you build a spatial map of where to find things).

Then we get to the book itself.

The thickness correlates with the digits written on each page to give us a sense of how big a 520-page book is or how small a 50-page book is, which helps us judge how long it might take to read (assuming we have read many books at this point). The weight of the book when we take it off the shelf confirms or helps us revise our guess. As we turn the pages of the book and watch the thickness of the already-read and the to-be-read portions of the book shift, we see our progress (tactile, hands-on experience with learning materials). We feel accomplished with each passing chapter. Our mind is imprinting the content and vital information from the book into our head with every turn of the page of a book (using touch, sight, and weight). If we underline, dog-ear, or use small book markers, we can create a way to easily refer back to the most important concepts. But most people can also generally remember where they read about something significant in a book by the thickness of the pages on either side and find the exact spot with a quick scan of the words in a given chapter.

Not only does a book give the brain multiple cues and information about its non-word aspects, it organizes the information and content while keeping a person engaged and feeling proud of the progress toward finishing it. And every time we get up to put the book in a bag and walk to the next destination, the brain is working on the information it was provided, consolidating and organizing with every step.

Now, as an occupational therapist fascinated with how the brain processes and takes in information, I find all this very important to know when it comes to the developing brains of children. As children, we, the adults of today, built our "reading muscles" and expanded our vocabulary each time we opened a book. The fewer the pictures, the more our brains began to visualize stories and information, storing it for later use. At the same time, the volume of information we absorbed increased.

The process of finding a book to read at the bookstore or library and the act of reading it provides an opportunity for the reader to have a physical experience with the content of the book. If the content of the book was broken up into short videos or provided as an e-book, there would be no spatial map, no size and weight to detect, and no white space to take a break and consolidate what we have read. There is just an endless amount of scrolling, one video after another, one digital page after another. Lots of visuals. Throw some ads in the sidebar or as a disruptive popup. Then add an algorithm that throws in a bunch of related videos we might like to watch when we get tired and distracted from the text we have already chosen. While we could argue that the library or bookstore also has many choices and distractions, there are no "popups" of additional videos or related products once we open the book or leave the library. It's just us and the book—white space, the mental space needed to focus, expands.

Is This the New Face of Illiteracy?

In America's efforts to combat illiteracy, the US has placed a focus on distributing more books to more people.[7] We got people to volunteer their time at libraries and churches to teach reading to those who never had the opportunity. We empowered people, regardless of age, to use their reading skills to learn about the world and understand laws and programs that others might use to take advantage of them.

Fast forward to 2024. I have observed on more than one occasion that there are still schools that are somehow graduating children that are illiterate (although the schools wouldn't dare say that aloud). Teachers provide videos and video games to teach information. School teams set up technology accommodations to reduce reading and writing demands for children who are struggling. Children with access to a phone, iPad, or laptop can easily watch as many videos as the algorithm populates, consuming but not absorbing and integrating new information into their thought processes. Rather than giving the brain an environment to ponder information and see how it fits with all the other things children have learned when experiencing the world, teachers provide information in short video soundbites, forgetting about the big picture, and teaching specific content that the brain doesn't readily know how to organize and file since so many of the multisensory cues are missing. This is not intentional by any means. Teachers are doing their best to facilitate learning with all the guidelines, expectations, and teaching tools that are in place. Kids may be consuming more earlier in life, but the volume of information is so great and in such rapid succession that the brain discards much of it rather than putting it into the mental filing cabinet and saving it for later due to its limited storage capacity. College professors are complaining that their students do not know how to read an entire book cover to cover, much less analyze the complex concepts contained inside.[8]

The result is a new kind of illiteracy. A world where attention span is low. The effort of reading seems way too high for a struggling reader when a video is available. There is significantly less time spent building the skill of reading during downtime. Many educators I have met over the years have accepted that some administrators believe that the most important thing is to help children access the content of the curriculum, not teach them curiosity for learning or build a bank of knowledge that will create the foundation for critical thinking later.

The world teaches us that we don't have to remember much because we can always "google it." Some teachers subscribe to this and only use open-book tests. It's a world where children's ability to critically reason through situations and learn about the world around them or learn about social dynamics is built on soundbites that influence our children but don't create a path for critical thinking and questioning, yet high school essays are still scored based on the student's ability to write in a thoughtful way about the content presented to them, write cohesive sentences, and demonstrate critical thinking on the topic. Writing is easily traded for typing when legibility is poor, but teens still have to complete a DMV application for a learner's permit by hand if they don't find it online in advance. Spelling is a lower priority now that spell check exists, even though understanding the origin of a word, hearing the word in a sentence, and hearing the definition of a word are all accepted options to help the would-be National Spelling Bee Champion win the competition. The SAT still expects that high schoolers demonstrate knowledge of complex grammar.

Some children are becoming exponentially frustrated during writing assignments because spelling requires all of their mental effort and they can't focus on the content of what they are writing.

Students are sent to universities relying on technology to fix spelling errors and grammar mistakes. How can you accept changes if you are unsure if the suggestion is right in the first place? You can only blindly assume. The ability to read and to write go hand in hand. The more you see a word and the more experience you have reading sentences others have created in their writing, the better you are able to apply the strategies of others to your own writing assignments. Hearing a word and listening to someone verbally explain something on a video is not at all the same as having many daily experiences with professional writers and storytellers.

So how is it that we expect children to gain the skills of advanced reading, writing, and thinking if the teaching tools and the accommodations wire the brain for a totally different way of thinking? How can we increase a child's attention span if reading for pleasure is replaced with scrolling to watch two-minute funny videos from the influencer culture? How can we expect a child to reason through experiences and improve reading comprehension if children spend much of their time outside of school laughing at funny cat videos, watching videos of other kids playing video games, and watching unboxing videos to show them what certain toys are like? We can't.

Were there still struggling readers before the world became digital? Absolutely. We would not have so much diversity in the jobs people choose if everyone did well in school. Plumbers and electricians bill out at high rates just for walking in the door, and they are skilled services that everyone needs. Some people do much better in occupations that require hands-on skills and experience, functional math, and functional reading in a chosen area of expertise. That's okay. In fact, it's more than okay because these tradespeople are becoming the new millionaires, and their jobs will never be outsourced to AI. What's not okay is not giving the brain a chance to grow and learn because there are Chrome extensions that can do the job.

Speaking as a Gen Xer, I think we made the mistake of seeing all this technology as a path toward helping us be more productive, normalizing the use of technology, and then reasoning that if technology helps us, it will help our kids. While certain types of technology are useful, they come at the expense of repetition, practice, and multisensory learning. The human brain thrives on this to build higher order executive function and critical thinking skills. Without this, kids remain stuck in the foundations of reading and writing rather than developing proficiency to use the skills of reading and writing to make an impact in the world. It's the new illiteracy.

Our community has embraced technology. There is no going back. Building curiosity and connection to the world along with the skills needed to effectively share thoughts with the world is priceless. If we constantly encourage children to outsource their brains to technology, the foundation of knowledge and experience on which all humans develop critical reasoning and problem-solving skills is lost on this generation. Unless we cultivate these uniquely human skills, our children cannot move from consumers to creators in order to harness the power of technology in a digital world rather than falling prey to it.

Before reading about the next habit, open your Family Playbook, and consider how you can enhance your children's multisensory learning experiences daily to create sensory-rich learning experiences.

Learn and Grow Habit 2: Develop Cash-Based Financial Literacy

Parent Goal: Your children will achieve financial independence.

Solution: Start with modeling how to engage with paper money outside the classroom, and give children an opportunity to practice this skill on their own.

I remember when Amazon's Alexa was all the rage a few Christmases ago. Amazon told us Alexa was basically a personal assistant. Ask her to help you find a certain song or artist and she could do it. Monitor your grocery list and prompt you to reorder on Amazon.com? Done. Search the internet to give you definitions and information about any topic you request. Absolutely. But there was a problem with Alexa that Amazon did not anticipate. Children learned that Alexa would give them anything they wanted even if mom and dad said no. Lucky for them that mom and dad's credit cards were saved on Amazon.com and Alexa was more than happy to pull out the credit card and buy enterprising children exactly what they wanted.

I never got Alexa. From the beginning, it just seemed too easy, and Alexa knew too much. What was invented for convenience to facilitate consumer spending on Amazon.com turned out to have some unintended consequences. Automated renewals of subscriptions to everything make it easy not to track our spending. Businesses reap the benefits while our bank accounts suffer the consequences of automatic spending. These are just two examples of the many ways that spending money has become too easy. And it's safe to say that post-pandemic contactless payments that also allow us to tap away money from our bank accounts have become the norm rather than the exception.

Many people never carry cash. There are infinite ways to pay someone without using cash: Paypal, Venmo, Zelle, credit cards, CashApp, FloatMe, MoneyGram, Skrill, Ria Money Transfer, BOSS Money—you get the idea. Exchange money with anyone anywhere. Keep your credit or debit card on file in the app, so the money arrives instantly. Save your card on your phone in Apple Wallet. Easily use mom or dad's Apple ID to purchase apps. Creators of AI agents imagine a world where your personal AI assistant will coordinate your appointments and spend your money for you as it pays for goods and services you request. No tapping required.

How Do We Help Our Children Make Smart Money Decisions in a Consumer Economy Designed to Encourage Overspending?

We need to help kids learn that even though money seems invisible and endless when mom or dad is using the debit card or Apple Pay at the grocery store, it runs out or debt grows. Children still do money math problems in school with fake money. Maybe you still play Monopoly with your kids or games like Robert Kiyosaki's CashFlow. These are all good starts, but it's not teaching the habit of digital money management and bridging the gap in knowledge between paper money and invisible money that is constantly changing hands online.

Learning about money from pictures on worksheets at school is not really helpful. Since the body is wired to experience the world through the senses, it is critical to encode the feeling of money into children's brains through tactile (hands-on) experiences. What does a dime feel like? How about a quarter? Bigger? Heavier? If they were in your children's pockets, would your children be able to guess what coins were there without looking just by the feel and weight of each coin? Maybe this is a good game to try with them. Did you ever stop to think about the fact that a nickel has a smooth edge and is thicker than all the other coins? Or that a dime is the thinnest, has ridges, and is the smallest of all the coins? Each coin has a unique combination of features that can be felt without ever looking at it to identify it.

Kids used to carry change to buy candy, soda, and ice cream. Piggy banks were commonplace before inflation raised candy prices over a dollar. Kids can still earn cash by setting up lemonade stands, recycling cans, walking dogs, and selling items at craft fairs. Children should use dollar bills as often as possible. They also need to see you using cash or, at the very least, you, as a parent, can facilitate them using cash and counting change anytime there is an opportunity to buy something they want or have earned as a reward. This process gives them a physical experience with money before they transition to money exchanges that are more theoretical. Teens need help understanding how currency relates to itself, how it grows over time, how it shrinks with every purchase, and that running low or running out means deciding carefully what you have to pay for or stop spending all together. It does not automatically mean going into debt.

I currently work with a young adult who is preparing for an eventual work opportunity. Initially, we made job lists for which he earned a "paycheck" so that he would internalize the concept of completing work for a reward. At first, the "paycheck" was a chance to bake something in the kitchen. Then we upgraded to a monetary strategy, using fake money. Life skills tasks we are working on were paid at 25 cents per minute. If he doesn't know how long something would take to complete, we use a timer and then calculate what he earns. Once his tasks are complete, we look up items online to see what he can afford to "buy" with his earned money. For this exercise, we agreed that the choices could be something to use in the clinic or ingredients for a baking project. His education is still ongoing, but little by little he is learning that his paycheck determines what his options are when he goes shopping on Amazon.com.

If you are saying to yourself, "Children need to focus on digital money because that is where the world is headed," it's important to *remember* that the entire economy is not, in fact, digital. Here are a few examples of why cash isn't going anywhere soon and why we still need to know how to write checks too. As a small business owner, I made the decision recently to stop accepting credit card payment and go back to cash, check, or Zelle bank transfers. Why? Because those are three ways that, as a small business, I don't pay transaction fees and can keep my prices lower for my clients. My transaction fees from credit card companies cost me thousands of dollars over the course of the year that could otherwise be used to pay my taxes, reinvest in my company, or take a much-needed vacation.

Many small businesses are cash only. Getting my nails done or my lawn mowed still requires that I have cash on hand. Even the car dealership told me when I got my car repaired that I would get a 10% discount if I paid in cash. Want to guess how fast I went to the bank? If it's an option you can take, who wouldn't want to save some money when inflation seems inevitable? Whether you own a small business or are doing business with one, cash is advantageous on many levels. Waiters still prefer cash at restaurants because credit card tips get added to their wages. The wage range for a restaurant server in Connecticut as of April 2025 is $5.72 to $22.41, according to ZipRecruiter.com.[9] The minimum wage standard doesn't apply because the industry itself is built on the assumption you will get tips. Coffee shops and other food establishments where you largely wait on yourself have cash tip jars. I also know of a summer camp that pays their camp counselors a fixed amount per week. Parents are well aware at this camp that tips are a must. It is advantageous to the business to have some of the earnings of the people who work for them be received in cash or in tips. There is no reason to think these strategies will disappear in favor of digital payments with face-to-face interactions. They are survival strategies for many businesses who are trying to lower expenses and maximize profits or income.

Paying with cards is so commonplace that fast food cashiers will hand you their credit card terminal at a drive-through before they hold their hand out to take cash. And if a young cashier finds themselves handling cash and they hit the wrong button on the register, that can create a problem of another kind. Recently I paid for coffee with cash. The change was growing in my wallet, so after I gave the 20-something-year-old cashier a $10 bill to pay, I said, "Wait! I can give you exact change." Too late. Her response? "Okay, just let me finish making the change and then you can give it to me. I am really bad at math." I stood, a bit stunned at this comment. Experience told me the cashier should either make change or provide exact change on a transaction. Has the vocabulary of money and transactions changed so much that for many individuals under age 25 this is a foreign concept? I let her make the change and told her not to worry about it. But then she stared at me and said apologetically again, "I am really bad at math!" Maybe she is, but this goes beyond just adding and subtracting. She had missed the entire concept of exchanging money in general. She was focused on the numbers displayed on her register. All I could respond with was "It's totally fine. Don't worry. The moment has passed."

This small moment will be etched in my mind forever. I have now adjusted my parent goals to make sure that my child develops financial literacy at all levels. She should be able to work in retail or fast food if she chooses, make sure she is getting paid properly, monitor her finances if she decides to run a small business, learn how to invest and save for the future, learn how to use a credit card without going into debt, budget to pay her bills, and save for a vacation. Heck, even learn how to be a savvy shopper, comparing prices, assessing value, and reevaluating over time as products shift and change. I am proud to say she knows how to compare prices per ounce in the grocery store rather than just total price. Once she started driving, I purposely told her she was responsible for her own gas. The price at the pump was a big shock, but it was also big motivation to bake more cookies to sell to her peers and agree to tutor another student three days a week so she could drive to school.

Some of the skills I listed, I taught myself as I got older and I am still working on learning them. I won't mislead you and say that children should know everything before they go off to college. Learning about finances is a lifelong process that expands as children develop and move toward independence—it's something to consider planning for. Be mindful as your children grow, so they don't find themselves in debt with bad credit at a young age and have no strategies to figure out how to recover from everything they didn't learn from a touch-screen world of "invisible money."

Since much of our banking and purchasing is done online, it is important to teach children first through the use of real money and then later through using digital records for tracking their spending and budgeting. Executive functions increase as children get older. Just remember that children need these multisensory experiences to build their perception of how money flows before they can move into managing "invisible money."

> Pause for a moment to reflect in your Family Playbook about some ways you can build financial literacy for your children.

Learn and Grow Habit 3: Be a Safe Driver in the Age of Screens

Parent Goal: Your children will become safe drivers.

Solution: Limit distractions and teach reliance on the senses over technology.

I remember the first time my mom took me out for a driving lesson. It was in the parking lot of my high school. No one was around. It took all my concentration to figure out how hard to press the pedals and when to turn the wheel to go around a corner, but I was driving, and this was the first step. I knew I wasn't ready to just jump on the highway and go on a road trip. I did not have the confidence for that! It didn't help that my mom was in the seat next to me, bracing herself with the handle of the passenger door and pressing an imaginary brake pedal. This experience is a rite of passage for many teens but also a major moment in influencing how our brains develop in adulthood.

When I learned to drive, the big question was: standard or automatic? The advice I often heard was that I should definitely learn how to drive a stick shift. You could "feel the car" much better. As I look back on my early driving years, I do wish that my dad had the patience to give me more than one lesson, but I think he was more scared of being in the car with me than I remember. I recall the timing of when to shift was really important as well as practicing not rolling backwards down a hill when trying to get going on a hill from a full stop. So what happened to all the stick shifts? They have become so rare in America that only driving enthusiasts special order them and pay more for the stick shift than an automatic. Some newer cars don't even have a "stick" to shift. They have buttons and dials.

In a few decades, automatic transmissions replaced stick shifts, there are back-up cameras, full-sized computer screens on the center console, automatic braking, and lane correction. Experiments with self-driving cars are ongoing. This means that parents are now teaching driving in the age of screens and high-tech cars. Seems like it should be easier, right? Safer? Not necessarily.

The challenge is that we are becoming passengers in our own vehicles, even when we are the drivers. Let me explain. Every time you learn something new, your brain creates new wiring and connections to make sense of it but also to build pathways in the brain to control the body, so it can respond quickly when faced with that new task again in the future. The more you practice something, the more efficient the pathways become. The secret ingredient to making all this happen is the information that our bodies send from our senses that provide information about how much force we need to use, how fast we are going, the distance we are from something, how our bodies need to be positioned, and where we are in relation to the world around us.

Let's apply this to driving. First, new drivers should never just get on the road and start driving. Practice in the driveway or an empty parking lot. Why is that? It's because new drivers need to practice which body parts and how much force they need to operate the different parts of the car. How easy is it to turn the steering wheel? How hard do you press the gas or the brake pedal? Anyone who has driven more than one car in their lifetime knows that this force is different for every car, and there is a brief period of adjustment every time you switch cars. It's brief because you have had enough experience that your body immediately gets the feedback about the resistance in the steering wheel and pedals, sends it to your brain, and your brain responds by telling your muscles what to do next. The first step in driving is really focusing the feedback the body is getting from the car to be able to control it more effectively. We haven't even gotten to looking where you are going yet!

The second layer of feedback comes from the vestibular system (yes, I need to get technical here), which, as you recall, tells you about your speed and direction of movement. As a new driver, 20 miles per hour in the parking lot often feels fast enough. Sitting as the passenger in your parents' car for 16 years, your senses adapted to the feeling of being driven and 70 miles per hour felt like nothing. But when you are behind the wheel, your body, eyes, and vestibular system tell you a different story. So new drivers are a bit more cautious as they learn about spatial judgment, speeding up, slowing down into a turn, and accelerating through a turn. In the days of the stick shift, it wasn't just about feeling the acceleration and deceleration; it was also about responding and timing gear shifts. Now that part has been automated and drivers should be able to spend their time focusing on the road, right? Not true.

Enter the third sense critical to driving—your eyes. You probably heard your parents say a million times: "Keep your eyes on the road!" And for good reason. Your eyes work together with your body and vestibular system to tell you how fast you are moving through the world in relation to other objects and vehicles. When you see something that needs to be avoided on the road or start slowing down to make a turn, your eyes see it first and your body responds to make sense of what is happening and judge how to adapt and respond. This is how a person learns. This is also what makes driving such a critical rite of passage for teens into adulthood. There is so much that driving teaches us about how to adapt to our environment and take on more and more challenges. Eventually, new drivers venture out of the parking lot onto quiet residential streets, then onto the main roads of town, and finally onto the highway where speed and timing become critical. If you are going to drive in a major city like New York City, Philadelphia, San Diego, or Los Angeles, that requires a whole other level of driving skill.

Several years ago, I worked with a 20-year old with significant cognitive and processing deficits. His family had worked hard to teach him many life skills. He owned his own lawn care business, with his dad's help to get him to the jobs. He wanted desperately to be able to drive himself and his equipment trailer around town. He harbored no aspirations of highway driving and knew his limitations. So we got to work in the clinic, doing exercises to build his spatial perception for how close he was to other objects and perception of speed. We used the Driver Focus App, so he could learn what to pay attention to on the road. Each time he failed a driving test, we took the feedback from the check-off sheet and created new exercises. These foundations prepared him to practice with a qualified driving instructor and, on his third attempt, he passed the test. For years after, he still messaged me on Facebook to tell me he was still driving and his lawn mowing business was thriving.

As certain parts of operating a vehicle feel more automatic by touch and perception of speed, more attention is available to focus on what is going on outside the car and to make judgments about how to adapt in traffic and navigate roadways. The better your children are at this, the more talented drivers they are, and most likely, the fewer accidents they will get into over time.

What Is Different about Driving in the Age of Screens?

First, the more automatic adjustments the car can make without the driver, the less feedback the driver gets from their body about what is needed to make those adjustments. The driver slowly begins to become a passenger in their own car. Second, the driver's eyes are drawn to the colorful screen in the center console because humans by nature are attracted to movement and novelty. Sometimes it's the scrolling message across the screen about the advertisement or the song playing. Sometimes it's the text message that pops up if your phone is linked by Bluetooth to your car. Sometimes it's the colorful navigation system with new instructions and the moving blue icon. Each time the brain detects a change or something new, the driver looks to determine if it's important. That's a big part of the reason that phones are wiring us for distraction.

All this means that visually, people are more distracted than ever, but their bodies have less and less need to focus on the physical act of driving because more aspects of driving are being automated. The end result? Having fewer things to do to control the car, our brains continue to seek novelty from the screen in the center console and the tendency toward distraction grows out of mental boredom. Back-up cameras are safer in that they alert new drivers on the off chance they have poor spatial judgment and are prone to knocking over garbage cans when backing up. And if you suck at map-reading, GPS just needs to understand where you are going.

New drivers haven't built the foundational skills of having a spatial map of the area they are driving in. They haven't learned how to read a map, and they may not be practicing backing up the vehicle without the use of cameras because the cameras are right in front of them available for use, so they become dependent on the technology instead of building the motor and spatial skills critical for safe driving. Car companies have assumed that people aren't going to be safe if they don't do it for them, so they keep looking for ways to stop giving them the responsibility. It's not that drivers weren't distracted before by kids screaming in the back seat, playing with the radio dial, having a conversation with a passenger, or trying to hold the road atlas and a hamburger while driving on a road trip. There have always been distractions. Maybe companies thought that making more things hands-free would help reduce distraction, so the driver could keep both hands on the wheel. Teen driver safety statistics compiled by the National Highway Traffic Safety Administration, reported that 2,034 young drivers (ages 15 to 20) died in traffic crashes in 2022.[10] Most teen driver crashes are due to three "critical errors": lack of visual scanning while driving, speeding, and distractions.[11]

Driving is the way that many humans expand their capacity for adaptability and processing multiple bits of information at once. When drivers become passengers in their own vehicles, the perception of where they are in relation to the outside world changes. The brain does not learn optimally because the sensory feedback is changed and critical connections are not built. Not only are they not built, but a mechanic told me that car manufacturers have now changed the body styles of vehicles because "blind spots" are removed by the cameras. So it's not even very safe anymore to only rely on checking your blind spots by turning your head because you might not be able to safely see the car coming up in the lane next to you. The industry itself is communicating that the skills are not necessary and technology is the future. Meanwhile, operators of bulldozers and excavators do not have computers in their vehicles. Why? Because companies know that it's dangerous and distracting. The liability is too great and the risk for distraction is almost guaranteed.

> If you have children who are learning to drive or approaching getting their learner's permit, open your Family Playbook, and review the strategies for developing good driving skills that are not technology-dependent.

Learn and Grow Habit 4: Build the Foundations of Time Management

Parent Goal: Your children will live independently and manage daily tasks.

Solution: Build a foundational understanding of time and space for planning and organization.

Do you ever feel like all you do is manage your child's schedule? You know when school drop-off is. You know when pick-up time is or the bus arrives back at the house. You know who needs to be at dance class on Monday, soccer on Tuesday, a playdate on Friday, and a birthday party on Saturday. Not only do you know when all this happens, but you also have expended a lot of energy coordinating the schedule so nothing overlaps. Or you enlist reinforcements for help, you leave work when you are supposed to, and factoring in traffic and travel time, you make life happen like a well-oiled machine.

What are your kids doing during all of this? Do they initiate getting ready for an activity on their own or follow through at your first direction? Do you have to dress them just because you are in a rush and you don't have time to wait around for them to do it? Do you experience a constant battle with transitions and getting your child to cooperate and get ready, so you can fit everything into the time allotted? If you answered yes to even one of those questions, let's take a moment to consider how you could make it easier on yourself while helping your children build the skills they need for success and independence.

A few truths:

- Most kids do not have an innate sense of time (except for waking up at 5:30 every morning when you want 30 more minutes of sleep).

- Most kids who have a lot of scheduled activities don't have lots of downtime to practice self-management of their time and plan their own activities.

- Most kids are not expected to use a wristwatch to keep track of when they are supposed to be home for dinner like back in olden times because many parents coordinate a pick-up time from a playdate with other adults.

Kids learn about how to tell time in school. They may even have to answer some word problems about time during math class. But now smartwatches allow people to do so many things that have nothing to do with monitoring time, that they actually interfere with time management rather than support it. Yes, you can set alarms and reminders, but that doesn't override the text messages, game alerts, phone calls, and step tracker rewards that pop up and interfere with focus and intentional transitions.

Practice the Concept of a Beginning, Middle, and End

In order for children to build a sense of time, they have to practice the concept of a beginning, middle, and end. A simple example would be that in order to play a board game, you have to (1) get out the game and set it up; (2) play the game (alone or with others); and (3) clean it up and put it away. Notice I didn't say, "Stop in the middle of the game to check a text or look up something on YouTube." Those extra steps interfere with children's ability to plan and sequence activities because they steal attention away from the task at hand.

The *beginning* involves the setup. Setting something up for children and just having them join in limits their ability to build an accurate sense of time. They need to be involved in the setup process. If the process is complex, share the jobs, and give your children one thing they are responsible for in the setup. Gradually increase the number of items your children can set up on their own to build initiation and follow-through. This is true for getting ready to get in the car, setting the table for dinner, putting clothes in a drawer, playing with toys, and just about anything else your children do throughout the day. Many kids are happy to let you do all the work, and sometimes as parents we take it on, not because we want extra work but because "it's just easier" or "I don't have enough time." The sad reality is, as Les Brown says, "Do what is easy, your life will be hard. Do what is hard, your life will be easy." Fast forward ten years, 15 years, even 20 years, you still may find yourself setting up things for your children and feeling frustrated as you hear yourself saying, "You are ___ years old! You should be able to do this yourself."

The *middle* is the time spent playing the game or engaging in the activity. This is pretty self-explanatory, so I will just say that even in the middle, there can often be lots of steps, depending on the activity. The easiest activities to practice setting up and cleaning up when your children are younger or really struggle with this skill are ones that are simple and repetitive but follow a sequence: (1) Get out the materials and/or change your clothes; (2) build, play, or engage; and (3) put away the materials and/or change your clothes. Tasks that are more complex may involve getting the materials but then require children to think or adapt throughout the activity itself, such as folding laundry or helping to make dinner, so initially children may only be responsible for one aspect of the task, such as folding all the washcloths or peeling potatoes.

When you get close to the *end*, prompt your children with time to spare to begin cleaning up the game before dinner or finishing the last two or three rounds of tag with their friends on the playground before it's time to get in the car.

Use Time Management Tools

I introduced you to the visual timer as a strategy for getting children to transition away from screens. Using concrete endings related to the activity—such as telling children they have time to go through the obstacle course two more times, hit ten more balls in tennis, slide down the slide three more times, take four more turns in the game—work well too. I have used both in my practice for several years and I can say without a doubt that when I forget to set the visual timer, my child clients always remind me, and then they check the time themselves to make sure they can fit in everything they want while checking in with me to help them create realistic plans. Now that doesn't mean that kids won't try to "add more time" if they are having fun or try to "make the time run out faster" if they don't want to do something. But they know it's not my only clock, so those tricks are easily remedied by setting up the back-up timer on my phone or in a place the child can't reach. Once it becomes familiar, many kids will actually set their own visual timers with your guidance and you can use a timer to help them figure out realistically what ideas are achievable in a given time. Teens and adults use visual timers too for focused work. The Pomodoro Technique is one strategy where adults alternate 25-minute periods of focused work using a timer with short breaks to increase productivity. Starting in preschool, this can be an easy tool to make time "manageable."

The second tool is a plain analog watch. Once your children begin learning how to tell time in school and learn about quarters, you can start helping them use the watch by giving them a time to end a game, a time you will pick them up from a play date, or a time they have to check their watch to know when it's time for bed. Make sure that you stick to times like 12:00, 12:15, 12:30, or 12:45 that fall on the quarter hours until your child can count by fives on a clock. Why analog after the visual timer? Because the visual timer is set up in a circle like an analog clock, where time increases or decreases according to the percentage of the circle that is red. With a clock, time progresses based on revolutions around the face and becomes an easy perceptual transition. Digital clocks don't reinforce the concept that time happens in revolutions, just like how the Earth moves. An analog watch is also free of distractions that, like ads on the side of a screen, interfere with the ability to focus on the task at hand.

Each of these tools gives children the opportunity to internalize the perception of time passing as well as encouraging monitoring of how much time is left or when a transition is approaching. If we just tell our kids when something is about to end and they have no idea where they are transitioning to because it's in the to-do list inside of our head, it shouldn't be surprising when they struggle to keep pace and have meltdowns. They are on the non-plan plan, and they don't see the schedule in their head to get there. As adults we often use many tools to help us organize our day and keep track of our appointments. But we forget that in the "done for you" world of technology, our children may not see a lot of clocks hanging on the wall in the community (or maybe even in the home) or the clock is cluttered along with other items on our phones. Children are often overscheduled as we seek out learning, movement, and social opportunities to help them grow, but we forget that white space and downtime is also time to develop the executive function skills we want them to have by middle and high school to balance their homework assignments and after-school activities.

> To set yourself up for success, open your Family Playbook, and think about how you can set up opportunities to build your children's sense of time for better time management.

What's the Bottom Line?

The skills for learning are dependent on multisensory experiences. The ability to engage in critical thinking and problem-solving, build emotional intelligence, and effectively communicate are uniquely human. Leaders and creators of today embody these skills. They have successfully created the technology that builds consumers and followers. To become the next generation of leaders and creators, our children need to experience many of the opportunities that generations before took for granted.

In the workforce, our children will not just be competing against people moving into America from other countries or people all over the world who work virtually. Our children will not just be experiencing shifting of job opportunities when manufacturing moves abroad to India, China, or Mexico. We live in a global economy where many people who aren't in skilled trades like plumbers and electricians or helping professions like nursing, therapy, sanitation, and law enforcement can do their jobs from anywhere in the world. But it also creates more options for businesses to hire low-cost labor from other countries, cut labor costs, and reduce the number of necessary employees by utilizing artificial intelligence, robotics, and computer programs.

Our children's main competitor will be artificial intelligence—AI agents that can complete full workflows with only one human overseeing the process and watching for errors. Artificial intelligence has made dramatic leaps forward in less than two years. Our educational system is not able to adapt as quickly as businesses implement new technology solutions. While education and government policy has always lagged behind innovation, the speed of change in the Information Age is unmatched.

Consumers don't change the world. It's how they think and behave that changes the product market. As soon as adults make it a priority to include more interactive learning experiences and real books into everyday life throughout children's educational careers, we will see a shift in the way technology companies market and do business. We still need books in middle and high school. We still need experiences that teach children problem-solving, resiliency, and sustained attention or effort to a project to get a reward. We still need kids to feel a sense of pride and accomplishment for achieving hard things.

The bottom line is that we constantly need to be asking ourselves as a community, "What is the right balance of using technology with our children and making sure their brains develop the way they should so that they have the uniquely human skills to be leaders and creators rather than just consumers in an AI world?" We need to make sure that our children are literate, can self-manage, and have the skills to blaze a trail, not follow the path that technology makes for us.

You have learned over the last several chapters that you need to (1) save yourself first, (2) support your children to connect and collaborate, (3) provide opportunities for them to move with a purpose, (4) and help them learn and grow sensationally. The final pillar focuses on digital literacy and internet safety. Thriving in a digital world means being aware of both the dangers and opportunities within, so children can master technology rather than become a victim of it.

CHAPTER 11

Pillar 5: Build Digital Awareness and Safety

Parent Goal: Your children need to have digital literacy, internet safety, and be able to make good choices online.

Solution: Figure out how to strike a balance between interactions through technology and connecting face to face for better situational awareness. Teach digital literacy and internet safety, so your children can make good choices and harness the power of technology for good.

In previous chapters, we talked about how to create connection with your children and how to help them build quality relationships with more face-to-face interactions. But as parents we also know that going online, at whatever age you decide is appropriate, will expose your children to a world outside your control. Whether you have children that currently have phones or iPads or will have them in the future, there are some critical things you need to know to protect them online while empowering them to effectively navigate the potentially negative or harmful aspects of the internet.

Since the internet became public, there has always been tremendous potential for both good and evil. After all, it is a place where people from all over the world and from all walks of life can come together for research, business development, networking, socializing, current events, and leaving their mark on the world. It's a place where no one is excluded due to race, ethnicity, gender, age, language, or beliefs. Sounds like a place that many laws over the years have tried to manifest in the real world, right? So why is it so important to have digital awareness and learn how to safely use the internet?

The internet was built by humans for humans and is run by humans. Generally, we can accept that we all are, by nature, imperfect. We can also accept that part of human diversity is that some people have self-serving intentions that lead them to doing things that society has decided are unacceptable. Can you sign up for a dating app and meet your future husband or wife? Sure. Can you also pretend to care for someone while you message them asking for money and take their life savings (catfishing)? Yup. You can. Can you join a mastermind group to help you up-level your business skills or get advice from people in your industry from all over the world? Absolutely. Can you also convince people to send you $5,000 via PayPal "as a friend" while providing little to no coaching for your fee? Yes, that can happen too. I can conveniently pay with a single click on Amazon with a stored credit card while someone in Nigeria is stealing my credit card information and selling it on the dark web. You get the point.

There will always be people with both good and evil intentions coexisting in the world. As much as we strive to protect our children from seeing and experiencing the evil parts, we have to remind ourselves that our internet experience is vastly different from that of our children.

It is important to keep in mind that the internet is still the Wild Wild West. As the internet became more widely available to the public, it quickly became a place to connect with others, share thoughts and ideas, and build businesses without having to go through the "red tape" of large companies and media giants to make a way in the world. Some boomers, Gen Xers, and millennials loved it because suddenly there was a platform where they could be heard. In America, we love that our right to free speech is protected under the Constitution. We love that as adults, we have the freedom to choose what we want in life. We have the right to pursue happiness. But at the same time, we struggle with others exercising that freedom if we are negatively impacted.

Societal Rules Don't Apply

In a virtual world and in video games, the rules of society don't apply. It's a breeding ground for predators who would take advantage of the most vulnerable in our society—children and the elderly. Children are more vulnerable to believing what internet users tell them. Lines are blurred between what is safe and what is not when they interact with others. They naively trust everyone is playing the game for the same reason. They trust people are the age they say they are in chatrooms. In some cases, there are rules and laws established in the real world that don't yet carry over into the Wild Wild West of the internet. Getting killed or raped in the virtual world isn't real, but the trauma of the event can be, especially when you know there is a person on the other side who created that avatar. But police don't have jurisdiction in an imaginary world. Anyone can show up in a chatroom, video game, or virtual world pretending to be someone they aren't. In real life, it's a crime to impersonate someone. Most of us have decided we enjoy these games because we are aware that it's fantasy and we are having fun making our own avatars. Generally speaking, there are a lot of fun and interactive virtual worlds that don't embed criminal activity into them. We, as adults, may enjoy meeting other adults in a virtual world, but we are appalled when we find out that a 30-year-old is "friends" with a 13-year-old and leading the child to believe that he is "just like him." There are consequences for carrying a fake ID and trying to get served alcohol in a bar. But there are no consequences for purposely changing the birth date you enter to gain access to a website or social media platform.

In 2023, the National Center for Missing and Exploited Children received over 12,000 reports of child sexual exploitation among its 78 million users on Roblox, many in exchange for Robux, a virtual currency used in the game. They also reported that child exploitation online increased on Instagram, Google, TikTok, Twitch, Reddit, Omegle, and Discord.[1]

As parents, we struggle with how to keep our children safe. We expect that there will be greater and greater privacy protections online to guard against fraud so that we aren't being "spied on" and tracked by government agencies or internet predators. But it is those same privacy laws that get applied to social media platforms where no amount of parental control settings will allow you to see what people are saying to your children inside a Discord chatroom or on Snapchat. How do we protect our freedom of speech while determining who should get censored? How do we preserve privacy online but also keep a close eye on who our children are spending time with to keep them safe from harm when social experiences are happening more and more online and less and less in person? There is no clear answer when adults and children have access to the same online platforms.

It is important to keep in mind that while there are cybercrime units at the local, state, and federal levels, they are often targeting the worst criminals. We rely on social media and gaming platforms to put algorithms and monitoring protocols in place for identifying harmful content and users that violate terms of use. Hopefully the Kids Online Safety and Privacy Act will soon be finalized and enacted. However, we should also recognize that those same companies have revenue goals, strive to increase the number of users visiting their sites, and use data they collect to draw in advertisers. The social media market will reach $251.45 billion this year, according to estimates from The Business Research Company and could grow to $413.6 billion by 2028.[2] As of 2024, the worldwide gaming market is worth an estimated $27.97 billion.[3] Similar to pharmaceutical companies funding their own drug research, there is an inherent conflict of interest in asking these companies to figure out how to protect children better. As I mentioned before, it's not surprising that the leaders of Big Tech are the ones who limit their own children's access to their companies' technology, knowing its capabilities and pitfalls.

With the growing mental health crisis among children, we struggle as a society to know how best to balance giving children access to the internet for all the positive things it offers and making sure that children are not harmed by the negative effects of technology. That is why keeping kids away from social media until they are 16 and not getting your 12-year-old a phone altogether are growing trends in America. Seventy-six percent of schools across America had smartphone bans in 2021.[4] Eight states have enacted laws to restrict smartphone use in schools as of December 2024.[5] Many principals in my local school district have noted that less time spent online has created space for more positive interactions among students throughout the day. While this is positive, we still don't have a solution to the dangers our kids face going online any more than we have a solution to keeping them safe from crime in the real world, but we can reduce the potential for negative things to happen and empower our children with the same awareness.

Are You Protecting Your Children's Privacy?

Parents are often the biggest violators of their children's privacy without even realizing it. Some kids have reported joining Facebook, only to find years of content on their parents' Facebook pages outlining embarrassing details of their life—tantrums, birthdays, bad school photos—all uploaded without their permission. For some kids, it makes them realize how easy it is for others to post things about you on the internet without you even knowing. For others, its permission to do the same.

Mommy bloggers post content, often not considering that people watching the content could be pedophiles, not just parents. One mom learned a difficult lesson when she saw a photo of her baby on an adoption site. As she recounted the story in an interview posted on Instagram, she shared how lucky she was that she was able to report it and that her child did not become a victim of kidnapping. Every year, parents sign media consent forms with schools so that schools can post activities and events on their social media platforms. Meanwhile, internet safety tips suggest that you never post a photo with background identifying information about your location such as anything with street names or names of schools in the background. These background indicators are the easiest way for predators to figure out where someone spends their time. Scary, isn't it?

We all need "situational awareness" when it comes to internet safety—that is, awareness of what is going on both behind the scenes and right in front of us when we engage with social media and gaming sites. We need our children to be more situationally aware than focused on getting "likes" and followers. As consumers, we are losing our ability to discern good from bad, marketing from real value and quality, and a scam from a regular email. We struggle to differentiate people's opinions and reactions to news versus factual events. AI-generated content can be created by known influencers to produce more content in less time, but this same technology allows for content to be created that impersonates them online and spreads false information. Even adults can't always spot the difference.

We are becoming a society that is easily led by the agendas of others. People who want to grow a business and make money build technology for that purpose, which can easily be used for good or evil. This will never change. That is why it is up to us to be educated consumers and protect our children in spaces where they can't protect themselves. It is also important to empower them with knowledge of how to stay safe online and when to talk to a trusted adult. To help you do this, I have put together a *really* short (not at all exhaustive) list of things to teach your children before they join online gaming platforms, start using email, post photos on social media, or order things online. Here's that list:

- Let them know there are both bad and good people on the internet. Your job is to keep them safe but also teach them how to notice when something doesn't feel right, so you can help them.

- Agree not to post negative videos and images about your children on the internet and consider if you should be posting something if you can't take measures to ensure your children's privacy is protected.

- Explain to them that they have no idea who they are playing video games with if it's not a known friend. That is why who they play with needs to be monitored by a parent.

- Tell them it's hard to judge someone's character through chats and text if they don't also know the person in real life.

- Acknowledge adults and kids both love playing games. Some adults make games that are not for kids, and your children may find them sometimes. Ask them to tell you when they find one, so it can be reported to the company.

- Make them aware that there are no social rules online. No one has to respect them or be kind. All kinds of posts, comments, and chat messages are allowed unless the person who owns the group or platform takes it down. Feelings get hurt.

- Explain that there are no laws in virtual worlds. If someone hurts you, you can't call the police in real life to protect you.

Better to leave at the first sign that something doesn't feel right.

- Talk to them about the fact that people may ask them to do things they think are wrong, offering to give them things they really want, like Robux, the virtual currency used in the game Roblox. This is never okay. Tell a parent, so it can be reported to the company, and together you can make a plan for how to block that person.

- Openly share ways to notice if someone is trying to trick you into doing something by showing kids email scams and suspicious posts.

- Show them how to review their privacy settings and location settings to protect themselves.

Explore more tools to educate children about online safety with the links below:

- https://beinternetawesome.withgoogle.com/en_us (This site is geared toward second to seventh graders.)

- https://www.commonsense.org/education/articles/23-great-lesson-plans-for-internet-safety (Common Sense Media is a leader in online safety education.)

Social Media Algorithms May Be Worse than Russian Roulette

When kids and parents alike consume videos, social media posts, and blogs from the internet, they often don't think about the business of the internet. They are pulled in by the entertainment value and in awe of the people who influence them. It's like watching a popular movie star in the 1980s. Sure there are more famous influencers than there ever were back then. There are a whole lot more people in the background with a desire to be famous. Noticed. Significant. But not a single idea of how to get there. Kids and adults create endless content, all in the search of significance. But not all of it is positive, healthy, or kid-appropriate.

Media companies will say that it's the "parent's responsibility" to know what their children are doing online. Senators across 27 states, however, beg to differ. The Senate Judiciary Committee held a hearing on January 31, 2024 including multiple social media companies and determined that companies have failed to police themselves at our kids' expense.[6] As I mentioned in Chapter 1, the Kids Online Safety and Privacy Act has been passed and is in the final stages of revision. You can read it in its current form on Congress.gov.

Meanwhile, attorneys general in multiple states have sued Meta, the parent company of Facebook and Instagram, asserting that Meta's social media platform features include the following[7]:

- Algorithms that are designed to recommend content to keep users on the platform longer and encourage compulsive use
- "Likes" and social comparison features known by Meta to harm young users
- Incessant alerts meant to induce young users to return to Meta's platforms constantly, even while at school and throughout the night
- Visual filter features known to promote young users' body dysmorphia

- Content-presentation formats, such as "infinite scroll," designed to discourage young users' attempts to self-regulate and disengage with Meta's products

I am pretty sure if you have a social media account, you probably agree with one or more of these statements, even as they apply to your own social media habits. A lawyer once explained it to me that it's kind of like handing someone a gun without a manual of how to take care of it or an expectation that they take a class and be knowledgeable in how to use it properly. While adults are generally accepted to be of an age where they have the legal rights and executive function skills to recognize these risks, children do not. Sometimes, we, parents, need to remind ourselves of that when our children are begging to get smartphones because "all my friends have them" and we don't want our children to be socially isolated.

In 2021, the *Wall Street Journal* published an article indicating that Facebook's own research showed that Instagram makes body image issues worse for one in three teenage girls. Among teenagers who reported suicidal thoughts, 6% in the US traced them back to Instagram.[8] A systematic review completed in 2018 by the *Indian Journal of Psychiatry* showed that online social networking leads to increased exposure to and engagement in self-harm behavior due to users receiving negative messages promoting self-harm, emulating self-injurious behavior of others, and adopting self-harm practices from shared videos.[9] I share these statistics both to alarm you and encourage you to make a resolution to fight for the mental health and well-being of your children. Make decisions that may be unpopular and inconvenient right now but will pay dividends exponentially in the future when your children are not just surviving but thriving in an AI-driven world.

The Video Scroll

On any given day, millions of people across the globe can be seen scrolling through Facebook, Instagram, TikTok, and YouTube feeds. There appears to be an endless amount of content available for consumption. There is no bottom of the page like on regular websites. No shortage of content. The algorithm suggests something that you would be interested in based on previous videos that have been categorized and populated. It makes it possible when you see a few videos on a topic to see a whole bunch more, which leads you to think that beliefs of one subset of video shorts reflect what the world thinks. Watch videos on positivity and personal growth? You would think the whole world is about growth and empowerment. Watch gaming videos? Suddenly it seems like most people online are gamers and getting rich doing it. That is how the internet is designed.

Google's data repository is massive. If you didn't already know, YouTube, run by Google, acts as a massive data collector. Using this information, they tailor content, video feeds, and ads to your every move. Considering how many people contribute to the internet every day, it's not surprising that it would be easy for Google to assemble a subset of that information so that you can feed any thought process (positive or negative) that you are having on a given day and convince yourself it's what everyone is doing.

The danger is that math is devoid of emotion. It's just math designed to increase user engagement and data to sell to would-be advertisers. It doesn't take into account the fact that maybe someone was having one bad day and watching videos about feeling depressed or breakups. It is natural for people to seek out ways to process emotions. Many of us do this with songs that reflect the mood that we are in. But even though we might binge breakup songs for a week, eventually, most of us as we go through the grieving process, start to seek out other types of music that helps us feel powerful, hopeful, motivated to exercise, or calm and relaxed. We use music as a culture oftentimes not just to reflect our mood but to change our state.

Short videos have started to replace this phenomenon. But because the algorithm is populating the feed, teens may not move on as quickly as they should to promote recovery and resilience. Teens can keep themselves in a place of frustration, anger, and hopelessness. Teens can find endless people who will never know them by name to echo and validate their feelings. While that can be helpful for a little while, it can also lead to wallowing in self-pity or getting "stuck" in negative emotions. Hence the birth of the coaching industry to save us all from the worst version of ourselves and inspire us to greatness. I am not against coaching. Just as you can find many things online that feed negative feelings and frustrations along with people to commiserate with, it's also possible to find inspiring stories, useful information, cute animals, practical advice, and things to make you laugh. But in order to fill your feed with positivity, you have to first make the decision to scroll past shocking and questionable content and the people that the algorithm is telling you are "like you." Your children have to learn to make that shift too.

While I am lucky that my own child has never fallen victim to content that encourages self-harm or eating disorders, I can say that when I notice that when she is falling victim to "the scroll," it's time for me to do a few things to help her break the cycle:

1. I practice presence and watch some of the videos with her on the couch.

2. I increase my "breadcrumbing." I send her positive or funny videos to make her laugh, so she knows I am thinking of her but also so that the algorithm starts changing her feed when she clicks on the video links. If you have other family members or friends that can do this, it is possible for you to create enough clicks to positively influence the algorithm.

3. I engage her in activities that require the use of her hands (like helping to empty the dishwasher, doing a puzzle, or playing with the dog) to get her off her phone. After all, it's hard to do more than one thing with your hands at a time.

Is this a fool-proof method? Nope. But it's a start. Talking about how I notice the shift in the amount of time she is spending scrolling through videos versus just telling her to get off her phone has also opened the door to deeper conversations about what may be bothering her or stressing her out, creating space for connection and collaboration.

The Negativity Effect

So what is my sensory and brain perspective on why we are experiencing a mental health crisis among youth that many lawmakers are tying to the impact of social media? I believe, in part, because it always comes back to how the brain is wired. The experiences we have either online or in the larger world cause our brain to fire and wire together connections that allow us to adapt to the world around us. Some of that adaptation is for survival. Think caveman needing to protect himself from animal predators. Scientists have coined a term called the "negativity effect" to explain this phenomenon.[10] The brain is wired to pick up on novel stimuli, detect changes, and evaluate threats. Activity in the brain increases more in response to negative stimuli than positive. It also readily focuses on, stores, and recalls this negative information. We have all experienced over time how traumatic events and difficult childhood memories stand out in our minds, but we have to search our minds to find the positive memories that we should be focusing on to develop gratitude.

The part of the brain that develops in utero after the spinal cord and brain stem is the limbic system.[11] This is the "prehistoric brain" that is hard-wired for fight or flight. It is what helps protect us from danger.[12] Being wired for negativity allows us to see potential problems, so we can make better decisions. If we are looking to buy a house, we notice cracks, peeling paint, and a dirty carpet. Realtors know this and always make recommendations to sellers to add a coat of paint to increase the perceived value of a home. Police officers are taught how to capitalize on the "negativity effect" to pick up on things that seem out of the ordinary while patrolling to identify potential threats and criminal activity.[13] Their experiences make them cautious and slow to trust because they have experienced the worst of people more often than others. The negativity effect can lead us to become hypervigilant to the intentions of others, expect the worst in people, and be drawn to content online that enhances the negativity effect in our brains.

Now that everyone has access to information, opinions, and videos showing the worst in people, it's not hard to understand how a mental health crisis among teens could evolve. Once you go down a content rabbit hole, it takes effort to change the tide because it goes against the natural tendency of the brain to seek out negativity and potential threats. Every internet troll comment, video dislike, or image/video that reminds us of a negative event can spiral us into a place of negativity, unhappiness, and mistrust of others. As children watch more and more videos that reinforce their negative thought patterns, the algorithm keeps providing even more. At the extreme, if children come across a video encouraging self-harm or showing others engaging in self-harm, a background thought on a really bad day can normalize the idea, turning this concept into an action plan.

If you notice a shift in your children's behavior, becoming more isolated and withdrawn, spending more time scrolling and less time socializing, it may be a red flag signaling you to reach out and connect with them. A combination of positive face-to-face interactions, reducing screen time, and "breadcrumbing" them by sending encouraging, funny, and motivating content can be a first step. But sometimes more direct intervention is necessary. If the strategies outlined above don't seem to be having an impact, always seek help from a qualified professional if you have serious concerns about your children's emotional and mental health.

Cyberbullying and Internet Trolling

The discussion of bullying has been going on for decades. Cyberbullying was at 55% in 2023 versus 19% in 2009 for middle and high schoolers.[14] The number has grown as more high schoolers have smartphones and engage with multiple social media platforms—TikTok, Instagram, SnapChat, Discord, and others—simultaneously.

A story that made national news in 2013 was that of Florida resident, Rebecca Sedwick, age 12, committing suicide after getting bullied mercilessly online by as many as 15 girls at once. She had already changed schools due to the bullying, but the girls found her again on social media. Her mother recounted that they said things like, "Drink bleach and die" and "You haven't killed yourself yet? Go jump off a building." [15] Two girls, ages 14 and 12, were arrested for felony aggravated stalking after the girls made additional posts acknowledging the bullying and suicide, but saying they didn't care. According to additional news reports, the 12-year-old was a former best friend of Rebecca, and the 14-year-old had supposedly turned her against Rebecca because she (the 14-year-old) didn't like that she, herself, had dated a boy Rebecca had been seeing previously.[16]

I would like to share a personal adult-version of an online bullying story. As a business owner and therapist, I post things online to educate and empower parents. Someone who was close to me created a fake "mom" profile to spy on my online behavior. I wasn't hiding anything or posting anything with negative content, so why would there be a reason to be concerned about what someone would see, whether I knew them or not? But later on, this person decided I was someone who didn't deserve the success I was having and decided that I should be discredited in any way possible. The hate speech ensued: random unrelated comments on my videos, comments in Facebook groups, photoshopped images, direct messaging to colleagues. I did all that I was supposed to: take screenshots, document the incidents, report the fake profile to the social media outlets, block the account, and delete the comments from the posts and pages I managed.

I am not going to lie and tell you that even as an adult the comments and accusations didn't hurt. I won't say that I was immune to their impact and could just step back when it was happening, writing that person off as being "crazy." It didn't feel good. And I was lucky to have a lawyer friend reach out to help me when she saw my request on Facebook for my friends to report this account for me. Facebook responded to my request, saying, "This account does not violate our terms and agreements," and, therefore, was not being removed.

Unfortunately, this story doesn't have an ideal ending. I wish I could tell you that the person targeting me just stopped. It wasn't the online behavior that led to a restraining order but rather the direct contact this person made with me in writing combined with a single European company agreeing to give me the IP address associated with obscene comments disguised as bookings made to an online calendar. What happened on social media was not enough to be a crime. Not enough to prosecute despite multiple saved images and pages of documentation. If I had this experience, I can only imagine what it's like for a tween or teen to experience bullying on social media.

Taking videos is a normal part of daily life in a digital world. We don't think twice about it. Meanwhile, I hear stories from middle and high schoolers about photos taken by friends who had a fallout being photoshopped and reposted online for public comment. I hear about kids taking photos of others in school bathrooms to ridicule children with autism who may be escaping to the bathroom from an overstimulating classroom. Now AI can doctor almost any image and create likenesses to make things appear to be reality, even without a real photo or video of an event.

Sometimes, as adults, it's hard for us to know what to say to our children about these topics. Children (all of us, really) are given an incredible amount of power in a very small and portable device. It's important to strategize on how to manage things that happen online, either intentionally by someone in school as bullying, as a conversation that gets out of hand, or when someone is impersonating someone else to gain your children's trust. It's also hard to balance understanding a child's pain over a situation with the realities of what legal protection is and isn't available online. As parents, this is often the time when fights with teens are on the rise as they struggle to create identities separate from their families. We are focused on them getting off their screens, doing their homework, getting to practice if they participate in sports or dance, and various other things that come with the "job of parenting."

However, we parents forget that one of our main jobs during this window of development is guiding children with love and compassion on how to navigate social relationships, helping them understand the difference between healthy and unhealthy interactions, teaching them how to face challenging situations online and in person, and also teaching them how to accept that there are and have always been "mean people" in the world that they need to rise above. We encounter "mean" throughout life. Sometimes when we get frustrated or are hurting, we become the mean people. It's important for kids to learn there are different kinds of people in the world. There are people who may say something mean or do something mean out of hurt or frustration but later are able to take responsibility and apologize. There are people who will never take responsibility and who repeatedly embrace the opportunity to hurt others. As parents, when we are the ones who hurt, we have the opportunity to model "repair" and reach out to our kids to apologize for our behavior while also asking for what we might need from them—like putting their dishes in the dishwasher. This can go a long way to build trust and connection with your children.

If your child has a negative experience online, ask your child what they are really feeling before you weigh in on the situation. Listening without judgment can create space for them to trust you with their feelings and be open to your guidance. I can tell you I felt hurt that someone was spreading lies about me. I was concerned that someone else would believe those lies, and it would impact my standing in the community and my business. I couldn't bring myself to just "block" the person completely because there was a part of me that needed to know what that person was doing. What were they saying? If they, posing as a parent in my community, were saying something that others actually believed, were they becoming more of a threat to me?

As already stated, most negative social interactions on the internet are emotionally painful but not illegal. They don't rise to the level of sex trafficking, catphishing, internet scams, etc. There are rules for these things. Lots of money is spent every year on initiatives to catch online predators and protect the public from true crimes. There are at least five pieces of legislation that have been proposed in 2023 and 2024 to support identification and prosecution around distribution of child sexual abuse material (CSAM) and exploitation as well as legislation that seeks to enhance law enforcement's ability to work with other organizations and victims to stop CSAM and online sex trafficking according to the National Center for Missing and Exploited Children.[17]

The police made it clear that, in my case, there was very little that could be done on the criminal side. While reporting and monitoring may get easier with the Kids Online Safety and Privacy Act, we are still a long way from guaranteeing the safety of children online. It took me a while to move past the experience, but I knew I had done all I could to take action against it. The next step was to just block and ignore. Once I stopped caring about the words, they just drowned in the sea of the internet. The same thing happens with every post eventually. People forget. Help your children to remember that if they are ever on the receiving end.

Emotionally Vulnerable Children Take One of Three Paths

Humans are diverse, not only in skin color or cultural background, but in levels of neuroticism, extraversion, openness, agreeableness, and conscientiousness. These variations in personality profiles can lead to emotionally vulnerable children taking one of three paths.

Path 1: They become victims of others, desperate for a sense of belonging and easily hurt by the negative behaviors of those around them. They experience high levels of depression and anxiety. They may adopt maladaptive behaviors to try to gain acceptance and love from unacceptable people.

Path 2: They become bullies. This can often happen out of their feeling emotionally vulnerable or because they come from an unstable home environment where anger and targeting of others keeps them safe from forming relationships that could hurt them but also on some level makes them feel important and powerful to counteract the experiences that make them feel powerless.

Path 3: They become resilient. People come into their lives that guide them through the hardships and help them learn that others' behaviors don't have to be tolerated if they learn how to set good boundaries. They learn that the person each of us can control is ourselves. They learn that while they can't control others or hardships in life, they can choose their response. Gradually, they learn how to establish a sense of self—to find people to connect to that bring them joy. They learn how to move through adversity and still experience a world where they can cultivate gratitude and happiness.

As a parent, your presence can make all the difference. As you grow your own knowledge of how to stay safe online, share it with your children. As you put in the foundations we have covered in previous chapters, you will help your children build resilience, learn how to connect with others, and build problem-solving skills. As your children build "situational awareness" online and in life with your guidance, they are more likely to become good digital citizens—leaders and creators—who add positive things to the online world rather than being consumers and followers who get victimized by the darker parts of the internet.

The age at which many children begin engaging with social media (typically starting in middle school) is also, developmentally, the most important time in a child's life to facilitate trust and compassion. As a parent, you know that it's a difficult and sometimes exhausting dance between establishing a positive relationship with your children that builds mutual trust and respect for open lines of communication, setting necessary boundaries to guide them in the direction you want them to go, and policing them as they get older and begin to create their own identities outside of the immediate family. Create a space where your children can come to you when things happen online. As a parent, you could reach out to the administration at a school. You could pull out your "mama bear" or "papa bear" and demand that the school take action against the tweens and teens involved. But what is the end game? Your child is at home, likely mortified that you "embarrassed" them by going to the school with the problem that they brought to your attention. The gossip around town spreads like wildfire and often contains modified versions of the actual incidents. Parents post in private Facebook groups that include educators, parents, and administrators. But what problem is solved? What is the mental health impact on your child?

Ask yourself instead, "What does my child need to learn from the experience? How can I level up my parenting strategies not to just save my child from the evil of the world but give my child tools to build resilience? How can I help my child learn from this to become a leader and creator rather than a follower, consumer, and victim?"

> Before you read the final chapter, turn to Chapter 12 in your Family Playbook to decide what actions you should take to help your children build internet safety and empowerment when going online.

Armed with the power of the Five Pillars, you can become a parent who is confident and capable of raising your children in a digital and AI world. It starts by empowering children with the ability to shift between harnessing the power of technology and showing up in a sensory-rich world to benefit from all it has to offer. I hope the book's final chapter will inspire you to greatness.

CHAPTER 12

The Winds of Change Are Blowing

Unless someone like you cares a whole awful lot, nothing is going to get better. It's not.

—Dr. Seuss in The Lorax.

I believe in the amazing creation that is humanity. We have unique qualities that can't yet be outsourced to technology. For example:

- The ability to learn about and experience the world in a multisensory way, unique to each of us, that fosters creativity and innovation

- Adaptability to learn new tasks and ways of being, based on a combination of knowledge and experiences

- The ability to create and imagine possibilities outside of what is currently known or accepted

- Emotional intelligence and a sense of ethics that influences our decisions and behavior when interacting with others

- The ability to sustain ourselves with resources from the environment without the need for electricity or other energy sources that machines depend on for their existence

In order to ensure that our children develop and maintain these abilities, we cannot allow their development to be truncated or derailed by a technology takeover. We cannot allow ourselves or our children to hit the "easy button."

With the many advancements in tech, we've made things "faster and easier" for adults, but there's been a cost: Technology has become a major disruption to family connection and the formation of deep, meaningful relationships. As algorithms drive our thinking, they expose us only to either what advertisers pay for or the next related video or soundbite in our personal feed. Our ability to develop critical reasoning and allow others to challenge our thinking has narrowed.

As I have shared throughout this book, research shows that the brain learns based on complex cues from multisensory experiences, including movement. Movement is both a key regulator for our emotions and basic bodily functions as well as a critical part of building connections to higher levels of the brain for thinking and language. Practice, experience, and manipulating materials in our environment has always been the mechanism for skill building, complex thought, independence, and creativity. Doing those things in a community that challenges us to work together for the common good fosters the building of social skills like collaboration, communication, and cooperation.

The digital world doesn't ask that of us. It teaches our children that they can have what they want "on demand" and on their own device without collaborating with anyone else. It makes money conceptual with credit, driving Americans deeply into debt due to, among other reasons, automatic payment of monthly subscriptions. Technology's "done for you" and high-rewards nature provides a false sense of success when many children feel like they are "failing" at daily life challenges such as relationships and independent life skills.

The point is children desperately need our help to ground themselves in their bodies while fostering brain development, creativity, and emotional resilience in the face of this incredibly seductive digital world. Left with their devices, children will likely become followers and consumers. With our guidance, they can develop uniquely human skills to become leaders and creators of their own selves and lives. They become empowered, aware, and deeply engaged in the richness of life.

Success Habits Are Critical

Success is no longer about preparing for a specific job or career, unless you are learning a licensed profession or a skilled trade. It's not about just making sure your kids get into a good college. Those can no longer be the primary measures of success. As parents, we need to do everything we can to foster uniquely human skills, trusting that our children can learn and adapt if we set up the opportunities.

It starts with us being present and intentional, not just in our desire to make sure our children feel loved, but in our desire to allow our children to struggle and problem solve because we know that it will teach them how to be independent and resourceful as adults. *This is Pillar 1: Save yourself first.*

It starts with simple things like expecting our children to do chores appropriate for their age and showing them how to be part of a family and community that work together. It's teaching them how to engage in face-to-face interactions to build communication and social skills. *This is Pillar 2: Connect and collaborate.*

It starts with being intentional about digital detoxes throughout the week while creating opportunities for our children to energize, restore, activate, and regroup through movement. *This is Pillar 3: Move with a purpose.*

It starts by empowering our children with the ability to shift between harnessing the power of technology and showing up in the real world to participate in things like sports, fixing a car, making a Thanksgiving meal, building modular furniture, cleaning the bathroom, and going shopping. This means that some of the things we have outsourced as adults to "get more done" might need to be sourced back to our families, so children build multisensory life skills for independent living. *This is Pillar 4: Learn and grow sensationally.*

It starts with teaching our children about all the good and evil that exists online while empowering them to make smart choices. This allows them to face the ever-evolving internet landscape with intention and discernment. *This is Pillar 5: Build digital awareness and safety.*

As I mentioned before, Jeff Bezos of Amazon is supporting the expansion of Montessori education, which is multisensory in nature, across the US. There is also a new model of education evolving in the private sector that combines two hours of AI-led online learning with four hours of collaborative multisensory learning. Are these models the answer? I don't know. Maybe for some but not others. But I do know that private entities recognize that our kids need something other than what they are getting in the current model of education—and it's not just e-learning to cover government-established Common Core Standards of knowledge. These ideas may take time to evolve, but many educators agree that the children they teach now bear no resemblance to those from even ten years ago and something needs to change.

If you tend to think in more concrete ways and in terms of societal rules, you may struggle to trust that these are the skills that will help our children succeed in a digital and AI world. But I have yet to find an expert on development, a business mentor, or a ChatGPT response that disagrees with the idea that the skills needed to succeed in the future are soft skills that can only be learned through the complex experiences that life has to offer our children. And we, as parents, are the ones that create those opportunities. We cannot wait for the governmental systems, full of red tape, to do it for us and complain when they don't. It doesn't mean we stop advocating. It actually means that we take the lead to be the voice of change in our families and in our communities. Only then can we come up with better solutions as the digital and AI world evolves.

For those of you with neurodiverse children, the road you navigate may have a lot more twists and turns. A lot more ups and downs. You may struggle more to balance the amount of time your children engage with technology. You may have children more vulnerable to tech addiction, mental health issues, and learning difficulties. As a sensory integrative occupational therapist, I can tell you for sure that the families who have empowered their children and expected that they could develop into the best version of themselves saw more growth and development in their children than those who didn't. I can't promise that your children will grow up to be "typical." That's not the goal. In fact, there are many neurodiverse individuals that have gone on to "break the mold" because they think about the world differently. But I can promise that if you follow the principles of brain and body development while working with a team of professionals, you can help your child become all that they were meant to be.

It is my hope that we can be intentional as we raise children in a digital world, so they have the ability to build the skills that research shows help people lead happy, healthy, and successful lives. If we let industry and consumerism drive the train for our children's development while adults and organizations seek out financial gain, then we place our children at risk for not succeeding in adulthood. We set them up to be consumers and followers of algorithms, not the empowered and independent leaders and creators we want them to be.

Remember what you are fighting for. Take steps daily and throughout the week to implement the success habits you developed from the Five Pillars. It's never too late to help your children succeed in this digital world. We create the structure, habits, routines, and experiences that allow our children to thrive. We just need to be clear on what they are.

As humans, we find meaning in our contributions and despair in our addictions. Seeking quick wins and immediate pleasure doesn't lead to long-term happiness. Long-term happiness comes when our core human needs of connection, love, growth, and contribution are met. Show your children that their family needs them. Show your children the community needs them. Expand your children's personal successes beyond the quick rewards of a video game to the greater rewards of deeper friendships, being a desirable playmate and team member, and contributing to the greater good of humankind. In that, your children will find their identity and purpose.

Any changes you make as a result of reading this book can only have a ripple effect. And, from my humble perspective, it should be for the better for your children and your children's children.

I believe in you. I believe in the movement I want this book to inspire. I believe that we can build a community of concerned parents that are chasing the same dream for all of our children.

> You have reached the final section of your Family Playbook. Use it to design a one-week plan to begin taking action without overwhelming yourself. If you have been impacted by this book, please share it with at least one other person in your circle and/or start a study group or book club if you haven't already. If you are like me, you never get everything from a book like this in the first read, and it's always easier reading and strategizing with others to build your village.

Endnotes

Chapter One

1. Schmalle, A. (2015). *The body activated learning handbook.* Stamford, CT

2. McGorry, P., Gunasiri, H., Mei, C., Rice, S., & Gao, C. X. (2025). The youth mental health crisis: Analysis and solutions. *Frontiers in Psychiatry*, 15. https://doi.org/10.3389/fpsyt.2024.1517533

3. S.2073 - Kids Online Safety and Privacy Act. (2024, July 30). *Congress.gov.* https://www.congress.gov/bill/118th-congress/senate-bill/2073

4. Rideout, V., Robb, M. B., VJR Consulting, & Common Sense. (2019). *The Common Sense Census: Media use by tweens and teens, 2019* (J. Pritchett, Ed.). Common Sense Media. https://www.commonsensemedia.org/sites/default/files/research/report/2019-census-8-to-18-full-report-updated.pdf

5. Engage the Brain. (2023, May 9). Helping your child navigate screen time. https://engagethebrain.org/helping-your-child-navigate-screen-time/

6. OSF HealthCare. (2020, January 13). Screen time for kids: How much is too much? https://newsroom.osfhealthcare.org/screen-time-for-kids-how-much-is-too-much/

7. Nagata, J. M., Chu, J., Ganson, K. T., Murray, S. B., Iyer, P., Gabriel, K. P., Garber, A. K., Bibbins‐Domingo, K., & Baker, F. C. (2022). Contemporary screen time modalities and disruptive behavior disorders in children: A prospective cohort study. *Journal of Child Psychology and Psychiatry*, 64(1), 125–135. https://doi.org/10.1111/jcpp.13673

Chapter Three

1. *Any anxiety disorder*. (n.d.). National Institute of Mental Health (NIMH). https://www.nimh.nih.gov/health/statistics/any-anxiety-disorder

2. American College of Pediatricians. (2020, May). *Media use and screen time - its impact on children, adolescents, and families. acpeds.org.* https://acpeds.org/position-statements/media-use-and-screen-time-its-impact-on-children-adolescents-and-families

3. Anderl, C., Hofer, M. K., & Chen, F. S. (2023). Directly-measured smartphone screen time predicts well-being and feelings of social connectedness. *Journal of Social and Personal Relationships*, 41(5), 1073–1090. https://doi.org/10.1177/02654075231158300

4. Cooper, A. (Host). (2018, December 9). Groundbreaking study examines effects of screen time on kids [Video]. CBS News. https://www.cbsnews.com/news/groundbreaking-study-examines-effects-of-screen-time-on-kids-60-minutes/

5. National Center for Missing & Exploited Children. (2023). *2022 CyberTipline Reports by electronic service providers*. https://www.missingkids.org/content/dam/missingkids/pdfs/2022-reports-by-esp.pdf

6. Atske, S., & Atske, S. (2024, August 12). *Teens and cyberbullying 2022*. Pew Research Center. https://www.pewresearch.org/internet/2022/12/15/teens-and-cyberbullying-2022/

7. Quizlet. (2024, March 27). Quizlet survey reveals students crave life skills education. *PR Newswire*. https://www.prnewswire.com/news-releases/quizlet-survey-reveals-students-crave-life-skills-education-302100754.html

8. Flaherty, C. (2024, January 10). *Survey: College students' thoughts on AI and careers*. Inside Higher Ed. https://www.insidehighered.com/news/student-success/life-after-college/2024/01/10/survey-college-students-thoughts-ai-and-careers

9. Bellassai, J. (2023, April 10). *Nearly half of college students don't feel career-ready, Forage study finds*. Forage. https://www.theforage.com/blog/news/forage-career-readiness-survey

10. Ruling Our eXperiences (2023, October 17). *2023 Girls' Index by ROX press release*. https://www.rulingourexperiences.com/news/2023-girls-index-by-rox-press-release

11. National Center for Education Statistics. (n.d.). *COE—students with disabilities*. (n.d.). https://nces.ed.gov/programs/coe/indicator/cgg

12. National Center for Education Statistics. (n.d.). *COE—public school enrollment.* (n.d.). https://nces.ed.gov/programs/coe/indicator/cga

13. Connolly, S. E., Constable, H. L., & Mullally, S. L. (2023). School distress and the school attendance crisis: A story dominated by neurodivergence and unmet need. *Frontiers in Psychiatry, 14.* https://doi.org/10.3389/fpsyt.2023.1237052

14. Kouvava, S., Antonopoulou, K., Kokkinos, C. M., & Ralli, A. M. (2025). Social understanding and friendships in children with attention deficit/hyperactivity disorder or dyslexia. *Behavioral Sciences, 15*(2), 216. https://doi.org/10.3390/bs15020216

15. Cocks, N., Barton, B., & Donelly, M. (2009). Self-concept of boys with developmental coordination disorder. *Physical & Occupational Therapy in Pediatrics, 29*(1), 6–22. https://doi.org/10.1080/01942630802574932

16. Bonti, E., Zerva, I. K., Koundourou, C., & Sofologi, M. (2024). The high rates of comorbidity among neurodevelopmental disorders: Reconsidering the clinical utility of distinct diagnostic categories. *Journal of Personalized Medicine, 14*(3), 300. https://doi.org/10.3390/jpm14030300

17. Kelton, K. (2024, August 14). *Living paycheck to paycheck statistics.* Bankrate. https://www.bankrate.com/credit-cards/news/living-paycheck-to-paycheck-statistics/

18. American Academy of Pediatrics. (n.d.). Where we stand: Screen time. *HealthyChildren.org.* https://www.

healthychildren.org/English/family-life/Media/Pages/Where-We-Stand-TV-Viewing-Time.aspx

Chapter Four

1. Reich, J., & Ruipérez-Valiente, J. A. (2019). The MOOC pivot. *Science*, 363(6423), 130–131. https://doi.org/10.1126/science.aav7958

2. Mason, M. (2022, March 7). How cohort-based courses can improve completion rates and impact of your learning program. *LinkedIn.* https://www.linkedin.com/pulse/how-cohort-based-courses-can-improve-completion-rates-matthew-mason

Chapter Five

1. Alotaibi, M. S. (2024). Game-based learning in early childhood education: a systematic review and meta-analysis. *Frontiers in Psychology,* 15.1307881. https://doi.org/10.3389/fpsyg.2024.1307881

2. Cooper, A. (Host). (2018, December 9). Groundbreaking study examines effects of screen time on kids [Video]. CBS News. https://www.cbsnews.com/news/groundbreaking-study-examines-effects-of-screen-time-on-kids-60-minutes/

3. Yogman, M., Garner, A., Hutchinson, J., Hirsh-Pasek, K., Golinkoff, R. M., Baum, R., Gambon, T., Lavin, A., Mattson, G., Wissow, L., Hill, D. L., Ameenuddin, N., Chassiakos, Y. R., Cross, C., Boyd, R., Mendelson, R., Moreno, M. A., Radesky, J., Swanson, W. S., Smith, J. (2018). The power of play: A pediatric role in enhancing

development in young children. *Pediatrics,* 142(3). https://doi.org/10.1542/peds.2018-2058

4. Altamura, L., Vargas, C., & Salmerón, L. (2023). Do new forms of reading pay off? A meta-analysis on the relationship between leisure digital reading habits and text comprehension. *Review of Educational Research, 95*(1), 53–88. https://doi.org/10.3102/00346543231216463

5. Statista. (2023). *Share of U.S. adults who read books in the past 12 months as of 2023.* Statista. https://www.statista.com/statistics/1402547/book-read-by-regular-readers/

6. Arundel, K. (2025, February 26). Only 56% of K-2 students are ready to read. K-12 Dive. https://www.k12dive.com/news/Young-children-behind-in-reading-DIBELS-literacy/741009/

7. Horvath, J. C., Horton, A. J., Lodge, J. M., & Hattie, J. A. (2017). The impact of binge watching on memory and perceived comprehension. *First Monday,* 22(9). https://doi.org/10.5210/fm.v22i9.7729

8. Thalheimer, W. (2006, February). *Spacing learning events over time: What the research says.* Work-Learning Research. Retrieved December 15, 2024, from http://www.work-learning.com/catalog/

9. Dunckley, V. L., MD. (2016, December 31). Children with autism are vulnerable to the negative effects of screen time. *Psychology Today.* https://www.psychologytoday.com/us/blog/mental-wealth/201612/autism-and-screen-time-special-brains-special-risks

10. Walker, C. (2024, February 1). Report: Predators target children through online games. *GantNews.* https://gantnews.com/2024/02/01/report-predators-target-children-through-online-games

11. D'Anastasio, C. (2023, May 2). Instagram, Google see surge in reports of online child abuse. *Yahoo Finance.* https://finance.yahoo.com/news/instagram-google-see-surge-reports-231347144.html

12. Rideout, V., & Robb, M. B. (2019). *The Common Sense Census: Media Use by Tweens and Teens, 2019.* Common Sense Media. https://www.commonsensemedia.org/sites/default/files/research/report/2019-census-8-to-18-full-report-updated.pdf

13. Quizlet. (2024, March 27). Quizlet Survey Reveals Students Crave Life Skills Education. *PR Newswire.* https://www.prnewswire.com/news-releases/quizlet-survey-reveals-students-crave-life-skills-education-302100754.html

14. Harvard Health. (2024, July 24). Blue light has a dark side. https://www.health.harvard.edu/staying-healthy/blue-light-has-a-dark-side

15. Korkutata, A., Korkutata, M. & Lazarus, M. (2025). The impact of exercise on sleep and sleep disorders. *npj Biological Timing and Sleep, 2*(1), Article 5. https://doi.org/10.1038/s44323-024-00018-w

16. Danish, D. (2024, July 15). The impact of social media and video games on dopamine regulation. *Philadelphia Integrative Psychiatry.* https://phillyintegrative.com/

17. blog/the-impact-of-social-media-and-video-games-on-dopamine-regulation

17. U.S. Department of Agriculture, Economic Research Service. (n.d.). *Consumer information and labeling: Food labeling.* https://www.ers.usda.gov/topics/food-choices-health/consumer-information-and-labeling/food-labeling

18. Lamb, A., & Lamb, A. (2024, January 15). Why are Americans so sick? Researchers point to middle grocery aisles. *Harvard Gazette.* https://news.harvard.edu/gazette/story/2023/12/why-are-americans-so-sick-researchers-point-to-middle-grocery-aisles/

19. Rainie, L., & Rainie, L. (2024, April 14). *The future of jobs and jobs training.* Pew Research Center. https://www.pewresearch.org/internet/2017/05/03/the-future-of-jobs-and-jobs-training/

20. Okray, Z., Jacob, P. F., Stern, C., Desmond, K., Otto, N., Talbot, C. B., Vargas-Gutierrez, P., & Waddell, S. (2023). Multisensory learning binds neurons into a cross-modal memory engram. *Nature,* 617(7962), 777–784. https://doi.org/10.1038/s41586-023-06013-8

21. Cooper, A. (Host). (2018, December 9). Groundbreaking study examines effects of screen time on kids [Video]. CBS News. https://www.cbsnews.com/news/groundbreaking-study-examines-effects-of-screen-time-on-kids-60-minutes/

22. Miller G.A. (1956). The magical number seven, plus or minus two: Some limits on our capacity for processing

information. *Psychological Review.* 63(2):81–97. https://doi.org/10.1037/h0043158

23. Bal, M., Kara Aydemir, A. G., Tepetaş Cengiz, G. Ş., & Altındağ, A. (2024). Examining the relationship between language development, executive function, and screen time: A systematic review. *PloS One,* 19(12), e0314540. https://doi.org/10.1371/journal.pone.0314540

24. Muppalla, S. K., Vuppalapati, S., Reddy Pulliahgaru, A., & Sreenivasulu, H. (2023). Effects of excessive screen time on child development: An updated review and strategies for management. *Cureus,* 15(6), e40608. https://doi.org/10.7759/cureus.40608

25. Ha, A., Lee, Y. J., Lee, M., Shim, S. R., & Kim, Y. K. (2025). Digital screen time and myopia: A systematic review and dose-response meta-analysis. *JAMA Network Open,* 8(2), e2460026. https://doi.org/10.1001/jamanetworkopen.2024.60026

26. Fares, J., Fares, M. Y., & Fares, Y. (2017). Musculoskeletal neck pain in children and adolescents: Risk factors and complications. *Surgical Neurology International,* 8, 72. https://doi.org/10.4103/sni.sni_445_16

27. Paulich, K. N., Ross, J. M., Lessem, J. M., & Hewitt, J. K. (2021). Screen time and early adolescent mental health, academic, and social outcomes in 9- and 10- year old children: Utilizing the Adolescent Brain Cognitive Development ℠ (ABCD) Study. *PloS One,* 16(9), e0256591. https://doi.org/10.1371/journal.pone.0256591

28. Tezol, O., Yildiz, D., Yalcin, S., Oflu, A., Erat Nergiz, M., Caylan, N., Cıcek, S., & Foto Ozdemır, D. (2022). Excessive screen time and lower psychosocial well-being among preschool children. *Archives de Pédiatrie, 29*(1), 61–66. https://doi.org/10.1016/j.arcped.2021.10.003

29. Zhang, Z., Adamo, K. B., Ogden, N., Goldfield, G. S., Okely, A. D., Kuzik, N., Crozier, M., Hunter, S., Predy, M., & Carson, V. (2021). Associations between screen time and cognitive development in preschoolers. *Paediatrics & Child Health, 27*(2), 105–110. https://doi.org/10.1093/pch/pxab067

30. U.S. Department of Justice. (2016). The national strategy for child exploitation, prevention, and interdiction: A report to Congress. In *https://justice.gov*. Retrieved May 17, 2024, from https://www.justice.gov/psc/file/842411/dl?inline=

Chapter Six

1. American Academy of Ophthalmology. (2024, July 10). *Screen use for kids.* https://www.aao.org/eye-health/tips-prevention/screen-use-kids

2. Boston Children's Hospital. (n.d.). *Vision problems*. Boston Children's Hospital. Retrieved January 23, 2025, from https://www.childrenshospital.org/conditions/vision-problems

3. American Academy of Pediatrics Council on Communications and Media Executive Committee. (2011). Media use by children younger than 2 years.

Pediatrics, 128(5), 1040–1045. https://doi.org/10.1542/peds.2011-1753

4. Witters, B. D. (2025, March 26). *U.S. depression rates reach new highs.* Gallup. https://news.gallup.com/poll/505745/depression-rates-reach-new-highs.aspx

5. Centers for Disease Control and Prevention. (2024). *Youth risk behavior survey data summary & trends report for dietary, physical activity, and sleep behaviors: 2013–2023.* U.S. Department of Health and Human Services. https://www.cdc.gov/yrbs/index.html

6. PBS Publicity. (2011, November 14). *PBS KIDS launches its first educational augmented reality app.* PBS. https://www.pbs.org/about/about-pbs/blogs/news/pbs-kids-launches-its-first-educational-augmented-reality-app/

7. American College of Pediatricians. (2020, May 8). Media use and screen time: its impact on children, adolescents, and families. Retrieved September 10, 2024, from https://acpeds.org/position-statements/media-use-and-screen-time-its-impact-on-children-adolescents-and-families

8. Konok, V., Binet, M. A., Korom, Á., Pogány, Á., Miklósi, Á., & Fitzpatrick, C. (2024). Cure for tantrums? Longitudinal associations between parental digital emotion regulation and children's self-regulatory skills. *Frontiers in Child and Adolescent Psychiatry*, 3, Article 1276154. https://doi.org/10.3389/frcha.2024.1276154

9. American Academy of Pediatrics. (n.d.). Beyond screen time: Help your kids build healthy media use habits. *HealthyChildren.org.* https://www.healthychildren.org/

English/family-life/Media/Pages/healthy-digital-media-use-habits-for-babies-toddlers-preschoolers.aspx

10. American Academy of Pediatrics. (n.d.). Kids & screen time: How to use the 5 C's of media guidance. *HealthyChildren.org.* https://www.healthychildren.org/English/family-life/Media/Pages/kids-and-screen-time-how-to-use-the-5-cs-of-media-guidance.aspx

11. Fleming, A. (2020, April 16). Screen time v play time: what tech leaders won't let their own kids do. *The Guardian.* https://www.theguardian.com/technology/2015/may/23/screen-time-v-play-time-what-tech-leaders-wont-let-their-own-kids-do

12. Bannon, M. T. (2024, September 19). Tech execs on smartphone-free childhood debate: Real evil is social media. *Forbes.* https://www.forbes.com/sites/marenbannon/2024/09/19/tech-execs-on-smartphone-free-childhood-debate-real-evil-is-social-media/

13. Bezos Academy. (n.d.). Bezos Academy: Light every fire. https://bezosacademy.org/

14. Zor, R., Szechtman, H., Hermesh, H., Fineberg, N. A., & Eilam, D. (2011). Manifestation of incompleteness in obsessive-compulsive disorder (OCD) as reduced functionality and extended activity beyond task completion. *PloS One, 6*(9), e25217. https://doi.org/10.1371/journal.pone.0025217

15. Nadeem, R., & Nadeem, R. (2020, July 28). *Parenting children in the age of screens.* Pew Research Center.

https://www.pewresearch.org/internet/2020/07/28/parenting-children-in-the-age-of-screens/

16. Dong, H. Y., Feng, J. Y., Wang, B., Shan, L., & Jia, F. Y. (2021). Screen time and autism: Current situation and risk factors for screen time among preschool children with ASD. *Frontiers in Psychiatry, 12*, 675902. https://doi.org/10.3389/fpsyt.2021.675902

17. Engelhardt C.R., Mazurek M.O. (2013). Video game access, parental rules, and problem behavior: a study of boys with autism spectrum disorder. *Autism.*18(5), 529-37. https://doi.org/10.1177/1362361313482053

Chapter Seven

1. Sweney, M. (2024, September 25). More than 9M play Candy Crush for three hours or more a day. *The Guardian.* https://www.theguardian.com/games/2019/jun/26/more-than-9m-play-candy-crush-for-three-hours-or-more-a-day-addiction

2. Stojanovic, M. (2024, February 9). *Gamer Demographics from 2025: No Longer a Men-Only Club.* PlayToday.co. https://playtoday.co/blog/stats/gamer-demographics/

3. Guest Author. (2023, February 13). *Five mobile esports predictions for 2023 from ESL FACEIT's Kevin Rosenblatt.* PocketGamer.biz. https://www.pocketgamer.biz/five-mobile-esports-predictions-from-esl-faceits-kevin-rosenblatt/

4. Ridout, B. (2019, November 7). *Dealing with smartphone stress.* Royal Australian College of General

Practitioners. https://www1.racgp.org.au/newsgp/clinical/dealing-with-smartphone-stress

5. Federal Trade Commission. (2013). Children's Online Privacy Protection Rule; Final Rule (FTC Publication No. 2012–31341). https://www.ftc.gov/system/files/2012-31341.pdf

6. Robbins, T. (n.d.). Do you need to feel significant? Tony Robbins. https://www.tonyrobbins.com/blog/do-you-need-to-feel-significant

Chapter Eight

1. Vogels, E. A., & Gelles-Watnick, R. (2023, April 24). *Teens and social media: Key findings from Pew Research Center surveys.* Pew Research Center. https://www.pewresearch.org/short-reads/2023/04/24/teens-and-social-media-key-findings-from-pew-research-center-surveys/

2. Sundqvist, A., Koch, F., Thornberg, U. B., Barr, R., & Heimann, M. (2021). Growing up in a digital world – digital media and the association with the child's language development at two years of age. *Frontiers in Psychology,* 12, Article 569920. https://doi.org/10.3389/fpsyg.2021.569920

3. The University of Texas Permian Basin. (2023, May 15). How much of communication is nonverbal? University of Texas Permian Basin Online. https://online.utpb.edu/about-us/articles/communication/how-much-of-communication-is-nonverbal/

4. Novak, D. R., PhD. (2022, March 30). Killing the Myth that 93% of Communication Is Nonverbal. *Medium.* https://drnovak.medium.com/killing-the-myth-that-93-of-communication-is-nonverbal-9603e5e6f939

5. White, E. M., DeBoer, M. D., & Scharf, R. J. (2019). Associations between household chores and childhood self-competency. *Journal of Developmental & Behavioral Pediatrics, 40*(3), 176–182. https://doi.org/10.1097/DBP.0000000000000637

6. Brussoni, M., Olsen, L. L., Pike, I., & Sleet, D. A. (2012). Risky play and children's safety: balancing priorities for optimal child development. *International Journal of Environmental Research and Public Health,* 9(9), 3134–3148. https://doi.org/10.3390/ijerph9093134

7. Brenan, M. (2023, September 25). *Americans' Preference for Larger Families Highest Since 1971.* Gallup. https://news.gallup.com/poll/511238/americans-preference-larger-families-highest-1971.aspx

Chapter Nine

1. Bigelow, R.T. & Agrawal, Y. (2015). Vestibular involvement in cognition: Visuospatial ability, attention, executive function, and memory. *Journal of Vestibular Research* 25, 73–89. https://doi.org/10.3233/VES-150544

2. Mastrangelo, S., Peruzzi, L., Guido, A., Iuvone, L., Attinà, G., Romano, A., Maurizi, P., Chieffo, D. P. R., & Ruggiero, A. (2024). The role of the cerebellum in advanced cognitive processes in children. *Biomedicines,* 12(8), Article 1707. https://doi.org/10.3390/biomedicines12081707

3. U.S. Department of Health and Human Services. (2018). *Physical Activity Guidelines for Americans, 2nd edition.* Washington, DC. https://health.gov/sites/default/files/2019-09/Physical_Activity_Guidelines_2nd_edition.pdf

4. Rideout, V., Robb, M. B., VJR Consulting, & Common Sense. (2019). *The Common Sense Census: Media use by tweens and teens, 2019* (J. Pritchett, Ed.). Common Sense Media. https://www.commonsensemedia.org/sites/default/files/research/report/2019-census-8-to-18-full-report-updated.pdf

5. Fincham, G.W., Strauss, C., Montero-Marin, J. et al.(2023). Effect of breathwork on stress and mental health: A meta-analysis of randomised-controlled trials. *Scientific Reports, 13*, Article 432. https://doi.org/10.1038/s41598-022-27247-y

6. Chan, S., & Debono, M. (2010). Replication of cortisol circadian rhythm: New advances in hydrocortisone replacement therapy. *Therapeutic Advances in Endocrinology and Metabolism,* 1(3), 129–138. https://doi.org/10.1177/2042018810380214

7. Ayres A.J. (1972). *Sensory Integration and Learning Disorders.* Western Psychological Services

8. Blum, K. (2024). The impact of chronic stress on brain function and structure. *Neuroscience and Psychiatry: Open Access, 7*(5), 262–264. https://www.openaccessjournals.com/articles/the-impact-of-chronic-stress-on-brain-function-and-structure.pdf

9. Hillman C.H., Buck S.M., Themanson J.R., Pontifex M.B., Castelli D.M. (2009). Aerobic fitness and cognitive development: Event-related brain potential and task performance indices of executive control in preadolescent children. *Developmental Psychology*, 45(1), 114–129. https://doi.org/10.1037/a0014437

10. Schmidt, M., Jäger, K., Egger, F., Roebers, C. M., & Conzelmann, A. (2015). Cognitively engaging chronic physical activity, but not aerobic exercise, affects executive functions in primary school children: A group-randomized controlled trial. *Journal of Sport & Exercise Psychology, 37*(6), 575–591. https://doi.org/10.1123/jsep.2015-0069

11. Sollier, P. (2005). *Listening for Wellness: An Introduction to the Tomatis Method.*

12. Blum, K., Chen, A. L. C., Braverman, E. R., Comings, D. E., Chen, T. J. H., Arcuri, V., Blum, S. H., Downs, B. W., Waite, R. L., Notaro, A., Lubar, J., Williams, L., Prihoda, T. J., Palomo, T., & Oscar-Berman, M. (2008). Attention-deficit-hyperactivity disorder and reward deficiency syndrome. *Neuropsychiatric Disease and Treatment,* 4(5), 893–918. https://doi.org/10.2147/ndt.s2627

13. Schaaf, R.C & Lane, S.J. (2009). Neuroscience foundations of vestibular, proprioceptive, and tactile sensory strategies. *OT Practice,* 14(22), CE-1-CE-8.

14. Terai, K., Shimo, T., & Umezawa, A. (2014). Slow diaphragmatic breathing as a relaxation skill for elementary school children: A psychophysiological assessment.

International Journal of Psychophysiology, 94(2), 269–273. https://doi.org/10.1016/j.ijpsycho.2014.08.897

15. Reddy, S. C., Low, C., Lim, Y., Low, L., Mardina, F., & Nursaleha, M. (2013). Computer vision syndrome: a study of knowledge and practices in university students. *Nepalese Journal of Ophthalmology*, 5(2), 161–168. https://doi.org/10.3126/nepjoph.v5i2.8707

16. Anderson, Julie. (2016). *The Impact of Sensory-Based Movement Activities on Students in General Education.* Student Research and Creative Works. University of Puget Sound. https://jstor.org/stable/community.36513868

17. Desai, D., Patel, J., Saiyed, F., Upadhyay, H., Kariya, P., & Patel, J. (2024). A literature review on holistic well-being and dopamine fasting: An integrated approach. *Cureus*, 16(6), e61643. https://doi.org/10.7759/cureus.61643

18. Fowler, C. H., Bogdan, R., & Gaffrey, M. S. (2021). Stress-induced cortisol response is associated with right amygdala volume in early childhood. *Neurobiology of Stress*, 14, 100329. https://doi.org/10.1016/j.ynstr.2021.100329

19. West, K. E., Jablonski, M. R., Warfield, B., Cecil, K. S., James, M., Ayers, M. A., Maida, J., Bowen, C., Sliney, D. H., Rollag, M. D., Hanifin, J. P., & Brainard, G. C. (2011). Blue light from light-emitting diodes elicits a dose-dependent suppression of melatonin in humans. *Journal of Applied Physiology,* 110(3), 619–626. https://doi.org/10.1152/japplphysiol.01413.2009

Chapter Ten

1. Gardner, D. P., National Commission on Excellence in Education, & Department of Education. (1983). *A Nation at Risk: The Imperative for Educational Reform. An Open Letter to the American People. A Report to the Nation and the Secretary of Education.* The National Commission on Excellence in Education. https://files.eric.ed.gov/fulltext/ED226006.pdf

2. U.S. Department of Education, Office of the Secretary, Office of Public Affairs. (2004). *A Guide to Education and No Child Left Behind*, Washington, D.C.

3. Carmichael, S. B., Martino, G., Porter-Magee, K., Wilson, W. S., Daniela Fairchild, Elizabeth Haydel, Diana Senechal, Amber M. Winkler, Finn, C. E., Jr., & Petrilli, M. J. (2010). *The state of state standards — and the common core — in 2010.* Thomas B. Fordham Institute. https://files.eric.ed.gov/fulltext/ED516607.pdf

4. Chen, T.-P. (2024, October 12). America's new millionaire class: Plumbers and HVAC entrepreneurs. Private equity is pouring money into skilled-trade small businesses; 'Next thing you know, you're running an empire.' *Wall Street Journal.* https://www.wsj.com/business/entrepreneurship/plumbers-hvac-skilled-trades-millionaires-2b62bf6c.3

5. Irwin, V., Wang, K., Jung, J., Kessler, E., Tezil, T., Alhassani, S., Filbey, A., American Institutes for Research, Dilig, R., Bullock Mann, F., RTI International, Barnett, M., Purcell, S., & Nachazel, T. (2024). *Report on the Condition of Education 2024.* U.S. Department of Education

6. (Report NCES 2024-144). National Center for Education Statistics. https://nces.ed.gov/pubs2024/2024144.pdf

6. Ludwig-Maximilians-Universität München. (2019, February 21). Signals on the scales: How the brain processes images. *ScienceDaily*. Retrieved April 18, 2025 from www.sciencedaily.com/releases/2019/02/190221122929.htm

7. AC. (2023, October 31). How Books Can Help End the Illiteracy Cycle in Our Country and Open Doors for Children. *America's Charities*. https://www.charities.org/news/blog-how-books-can-help-end-illiteracy-cycle-our-country-and-open-doors-children/

8. Horowitch, R. (2024, October 2). The elite college students who can't read books. *The Atlantic*. https://www.theatlantic.com/magazine/archive/2024/11/the-elite-college-students-who-cant-read-books/679945/

9. Restaurant Server Salary in Connecticut. (n.d.). ZipRecruiter.com. Retrieved April 14, 2025, from https://www.ziprecruiter.com/Salaries/Restaurant-Server-Salary-in-Connecticut

10. National Highway and Transportation Safety Administration: National Center for Statistics and Analysis. (2024). Traffic Safety Facts 2022 data: *Young drivers*. U.S. Department of Transportation. https://crashstats.nhtsa.dot.gov/

11. Curry, A. E., Hafetz, J., Kallan, M. J., Winston, F. K., & Durbin, D. R. (2011). Prevalence of teen driver errors leading to serious motor vehicle crashes. *Accident Analysis &*

Prevention, 43(4), 1285–1290. https://doi.org/10.1016/j.aap.2010.10.019

Chapter Eleven

1. D'Anastasio, C. (2023, May 2). Instagram, Google see surge in reports of online child abuse. *Yahoo Finance*. https://finance.yahoo.com/news/instagram-google-see-surge-reports-231347144.html

2. The Business Research Company. (2025). *Social Media Global Market Report 2025*. https://www.thebusinessresearchcompany.com/report/social-media-global-market-report

3. Baker, N. (2024, September 12). Online Gaming Statistics 2024 Report - Online Gaming Facts and Stats. *Uswitch*. https://www.uswitch.com/broadband/studies/online-gaming-statistics/

4. Gometz, E. (2024b, September 27). What research shows about smartphone bans in schools. *Science Friday*. https://www.sciencefriday.com/segments/smartphone-ban-in-schools/

5. Sequeira, R (2025, February 24). *School cellphone bans spread across states, Though enforcement could be tricky: The research on social media's harmful effects has moved lawmakers to bipartisan action.* Stateline. Retrieved April 1, 2025 from https://stateline.org/2025/02/24/school-cellphone-bans-spread-across-states-though-enforcement-could-be-tricky/

6. Mapa, K. (n.d.). Senate Judiciary Hearing about Online Safety – CWLA. https://www.cwla.org/senate-judiciary-hearing-about-online-safety/

7. Brown, C. S. (2024, February 20). Here's why states are suing meta for hurting teens with Facebook and Instagram. *Scientific American.* https://www.scientificamerican.com/article/heres-why-states-are-suing-meta-for-hurting-teens-with-facebook-and-instagram/

8. Wells, Howritz, Seetharaman, G., Jeff, Deepa. (2021). Facebook knows Instagram Is toxic for teen girls, Company documents show. *The Wall Street Journal.* https://www.wsj.com/articles/facebook-knows-instagram-is-toxic-for-teen-girls-company-documents-show-11631620739

9. Memon, A., Sharma, S., Mohite, S., & Jain, S. (2018). The role of online social networking on deliberate self-harm and suicidality in adolescents: A systematized review of literature. *Indian Journal of Psychiatry,* 60(4), 384. https://doi.org/10.4103/psychiatry.indianjpsychiatry_414_17

10. Lazarus, J. (2021). Negativity bias: An evolutionary hypothesis and an empirical programme. *Learning and Motivation,* 75, 101731. https://doi.org/10.1016/j.lmot.2021.101731

11. Vasung, L., Abaci Turk, E., Ferradal, S. L., Sutin, J., Stout, J. N., Ahtam, B., Lin, P. Y., & Grant, P. E. (2019). Exploring early human brain development with structural and physiological neuroimaging. *NeuroImage,* 187, 226–254. https://doi.org/10.1016/j.neuroimage.2018.07.041

12. Howard E. LeWine, MD (Ed.). (2024, April 3). Understanding the stress response: Chronic activation of this survival mechanism impairs health. *Harvard*

Health Publishing. https://www.health.harvard.edu/staying-healthy/understanding-the-stress-response

13. Gastelum, J. (2021, January 18). How negativity bias can impact a police officer's home life. *Police1*. https://www.police1.com/health-fitness/articles/why-our-brains-fixate-on-the-bad-and-what-to-do-about-it-hU18RitjpIsT4Moe/

14. Cyberbullying Research Center. (2025, June 30). *Summary of our cyberbullying research* (2004-2022). cyberbullying.org. https://cyberbullying.org/summary-of-our-cyberbullying-research

15. Miller, M. (2013, September 17). Bullies use social media to urge 12 year-old to kill herself. *cbsnews.com*. CBS News. Retrieved May 10 2025, from https://www.cbsnews.com/news/bullies-use-social-media-to-urge-12-year-old-to-kill-herself/.

16. Associated Press. (2013, October 15). Rebecca Ann Sedwick suicide: 2 arrests made in death of bullied Florida girl. *cbsnews.com*. CBS News. Retrieved May 10 2025, from https://www.cbsnews.com/news/rebecca-ann-sedwick-suicide-2-arrests-made-in-death-of-bullied-florida-girl/

17. Survivors speak out in support of critical child protection legislation. (n.d.) (2023). *missingkids.org*. National Center for Missing & Exploited Children. https://www.missingkids.org/blog/2023/survivors-speak-out-in-support-of-critical-child-protection-legislation

Acknowledgments

My daughter—Through all of life's ups and downs, what I couldn't do for myself, I did for you. You are the reason I have always pushed myself to grow intentionally and become the mom that you needed most at any given point in your life. You are the reason I created a business where I could always be there for you when it mattered most. You are the reason that I started the journey of personal growth and achievement. You are the reason I was able to take uncomfortable action. While I know I am imperfect, I hope that both my scars and my healing journey have modeled to you that growth is possible and you can do anything if you act with intention and choose to build people up who can leave the world a better place.

My true friends—Danette, Kara, Cassandra, Marilyn, Rachel, and Michelle. While most of you have come into my life in adulthood, you have always been the voices in my head supporting me and reminding me that I can do anything. There were days that I felt not good enough, you accepted me and supported me anyway. You allowed me to be your guide when you needed professional advice, and you were my guides too, personally and professionally.

My family—While my father is not here to see this book published, he was always secretly my biggest fan. Thank you, Mom, for listening as I processed my thoughts about the world, parenting, and the path forward. Thank you for letting me think out loud and helping me solidify my "why." Thank you, Roger and Michael, for spirited conversations and teaching me to speak up for my beliefs if I want to be heard.

The families I work with—You are my inspiration. The success of your children inspires me to keep growing my skills and adapting to meet the needs of a digital generation. Your desire to help your own children find happiness and success and your commitment to the process gives me the energy to persevere. When any of your children walk out of a therapy session standing taller and prouder than when they went in, my heart soars and I know I have made a difference.

I am so grateful to all the people who have influenced the direction of my life and the experiences that have shaped me into the person I am. Even if I haven't mentioned you by name, please know that.

About the Author

Aubrey Schmalle, OTR/L, SIPT, is a nationally recognized occupational therapist and the creator of the *Body Activated Learning*^{TM} framework. With over two decades of experience specializing in sensory integration, Aubrey has helped thousands of children and families bridge the gap between therapy and real life—empowering them to thrive in today's fast-paced, digital world.

A passionate educator and sought-after speaker, Aubrey brings science-backed strategies and compassionate guidance to parents, educators, and professionals nationwide. Her work is grounded in neuroscience, yet always rooted in connection, creativity, and the realities of daily family life.

When she's not working with clients or writing, Aubrey is a proud mom to a Gen Z teen and a devoted dog mom to Cooper, a mischievous poochon. She finds balance through movement, creativity, and her latest passion project—reviving a wild backyard garden, one bloom at a time.

www.ingramcontent.com/pod-product-compliance
Lightning Source LLC
Chambersburg PA
CBHW052016070526
44584CB00016B/1778